CANDLES

for the

DEFIANT

*Discovering my Family's
Estonian Past*

KAIA GALLAGHER

Published in the United States by:
Atterberry Press
Centennial, Colorado
All rights reserved

Publisher's Cataloging-in-Publication Data

Names: Gallagher, Kaia, 1950- .
Title: Candles for the defiant : discovering my family's Estonian past / Kaia Gallagher.
Description: Centennial, CO : Atterberry Press, 2024. | Includes 18 b&cw illustrations: photos, map, family tree. | Includes bibliographical references. | Summary: During her search to learn more about her family's Estonian past, Kaia uncovers the efforts of a would-be uncle who resisted the Soviet occupation of Estonia during World War II only to later be condemned as a traitor and a spy when Estonia was occupied by the Germans in 1942.
Identifiers: LCCN 2023948230 | ISBN 9798989203604 (pbk) | ISBN 9798989203611 (ebook) | ISBN 9798989203628 (audio)
Subjects: LCSH: Kull, Bruno Kulgma, 1914-1942. | Vares, Asta, 1919-1942. | Gallagher, Kaia Vares, 1921-2018. | Gallagher, Kaia, 1950- . | Estonia – History – Soviet occupation 1940-1941. | Estonia – History – German occupation 1941-1944. | World War, 1939-1945—Estonia. | BISAC: HISTORY / Europe / Baltic States. | HISTORY / Wars & Conflicts / World War II / Eastern Front. | BIOGRAPHY & AUTOBIOGRAPHY / Historical.
Classification: LCC D802.E75 G35 2024 | DDC 947.9808--dc23
LC record available at https://lccn.loc.gov/2023948230

Cover and Interior Design by 100 Covers

For rights and permissions, please contact:

Kaia Gallagher
7934 South Clayton Circle
Centennial, Colorado 80122
Kaia@kaiagallagher.com

For my mother whose courage and determination
continues to inspire me

Contents

Map of Estonia

Source: U.S. Department of State

A Timeline of Estonian History

98 A.D.	Roman historian Tacitus writes about the "aesti" tribes in his book *Germania.*
1211	The crusading Livonian Brothers of the Sword conquer Estonia.
1582	Southern Estonia is incorporated into the state of Poland-Lithuania.
1625	Swedes take control of Tartu and Southern Estonia.
1710	After the Great Northern War, Estonia is incorporated into the Russian Empire.
1819	Serfdom is abolished.
1918	Bolshevist Soviet Russian forces move against Estonia.
1918	Estonia issues a Declaration of Independence.
1918-1920	Estonia fights for its independence from Soviet Russia.
1920	Russia acknowledges Estonian sovereignty in the Treaty of Tartu.
1922	Estonia joins the League of Nations.
1939	The Soviet Union demands the right to build military bases on Estonian territory after the Molotov-Ribbentrop Pact is signed by Germany and the Soviet Union.
1940	The Red Army occupies Estonia on June 17. Estonia is unlawfully incorporated into the Soviet Union on August 6.
1941	The Soviet Union initiates a mass deportation in the Baltic states on June 14.

Germany invades the U.S.S.R. on June 22 and occupies Estonia on December 1.

1944   The Soviet Union crosses the Estonian border on January 30.

The Soviets capture Tartu on August 26.

The Soviet Union takes control of all of Estonia on September 22.

1949   The Soviet Union conducts a second mass deportation in Estonia on March 25.

1989   Two million Baltic citizens join hands to demand independence for the Baltic States.

1991   The Soviet Union recognizes Estonian independence from the U.S.S.R.

1992   Lennart Meri is elected President of Estonia.

1994   The Russian army leaves Estonia.[1]

---

1   "Timeline of Estonian History," Wikipedia.

Vares Family Tree

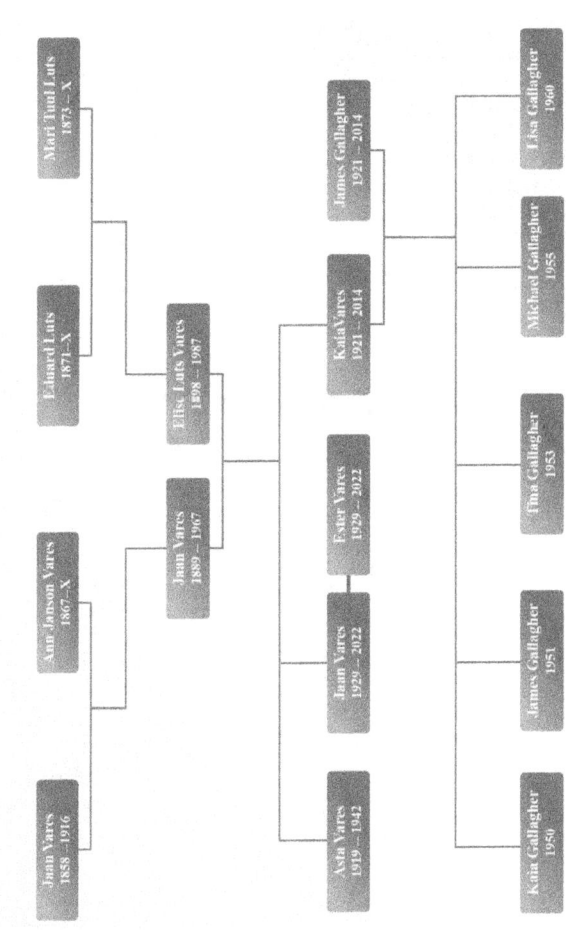

Author's Note

Despite being half-Estonian and having an Estonian first name, I have spent nearly a lifetime seeking to understand my Estonian heritage. After my mother and her family escaped from Estonia at the end of World War II, they chose to leave behind the trauma they experienced. Yet, without knowing the family stories they were reluctant to share, I felt as if part of myself was missing.

I visited Estonia for the first time in 1985 when I was 35. Since that first trip, I returned in 2005 and again in 2018. Each time, I learned more about my family's struggle to survive when Estonia was taken over by the Soviets in 1939, by the Germans in 1941, and then again by the Soviets in 1944 for a postwar occupation that would last for nearly fifty years.

This family memoir is a work of nonfiction. To the best of my abilities, I have recreated my mother's stories about her life in Estonia, her escape from her homeland, and her experiences during World War II. I have also relied on family records, photo albums, and letters to chronicle my family's narrative.

My brother, Michael, who lives in Estonia, has been a tremendous resource and helped me to access family-related files dating from the war years that were preserved by the Estonian National Archives. The endnotes provided at the back of this book identify other reference documents and historical accounts I have used as source materials.

Many Estonian families have stories to tell regarding how their relatives suffered during World War II. Estonia's wartime history also includes narratives that detail how patriotic Estonians sacrificed their lives to defend their country's independence. The courage and stubborn determination of these patriots provided a foundation that helped to keep Estonia's dreams of independence alive for nearly five decades until the country was able to reestablish itself as a democratic nation in 1991. My family's story is part of this remarkable history.

CHAPTER 1

THE GHOST AMONG US

Her name was Asta and she died when she was only twenty-two years old. Her symptoms suggested she suffered from an aggressive form of cancer, but my mother always believed her older sister died from a broken heart. In 1940, during the early years of World War II, when my grandparents debated whether they should try to escape from Estonia, Asta was adamant. She would never leave without her fiancée, Bruno. Two years later, they would both be dead.

As World War II was coming to an end in 1944, Mom and her family managed to escape a day before the Soviets occupied Estonia for the next five decades. They left behind the life they once lived and the country they loved, but never let go of their memories of Asta, the idealistic young woman whose dreams for the future died when her fiancée was executed by the Germans.

I was five years old when I first noticed Asta's black and white photograph hanging in my grandmother's front hall. It was 1955 and by that time World War II had been over for more than ten years. Puzzled to discover there could be anyone among the constellation of family photos I did not recognize, I asked my mother who she was.

In response, my grandmother, who was standing nearby, covered her face with both hands and started to sob while my mother whisked me away and told me not to ask so many questions. I was too young to understand what I had done or why my grandmother had become upset, but I learned that day that my family had painful secrets from the past, secrets that no one wanted to discuss.

It was five years later, when, at the age of ten, I first learned Asta's name. On a summer afternoon, while my grandparents were visiting, I tried out a rope swing, hit a tree, and suffered a concussion. Worried that I might be seriously injured, my grandfather, who was a physician, sat by my bedside to watch for any changes in my condition. As he sat in my darkened bedroom, he became lost in his thoughts and, forgetting where he was, called out "Aaastaaa" in an agonizing sob. Awakened by his cry, I watched as he got up from his chair and quickly shuffled out of my bedroom. When my mother came to see how I was doing, I asked, "What does the word Asta mean?"

"Why are you asking me this?"

"I heard Grandpop call out that word. What does it mean?"

Mom sighed and said, "Asta was my sister."

"You have a sister? How come you never told me?"

As she turned to leave the room, Mom said over her shoulder, "She died. Don't ask me about this."

On that lazy summer day when my grandfather sat by my bedside and called out Asta's name, nearly twenty years had gone by since his first-born child had died. Yet while he watched over me, he must have been transported back to a time when he knew that his daughter's health was steadily declining. He would also have been aware there was nothing he could do to keep her alive. Despite the decades of time that had passed by, the grief he experienced never seemed to have diminished.

My grandmother also held onto the memory of her oldest daughter. Although I never heard her talk about Asta, I later discovered that she compiled a pocket photo album in which she preserved pictures from her daughter's life. Starting with joyful scenes of Asta as a smiling infant, the album pages showed her to be a bubbly toddler who grew into an inquisitive tomboy and later a svelte teenager. Asta's gravesite filled the last photo frame, a final statement that punctuated her short life. How often did my grandmother scan through the album, I wondered, particularly during the many years when she was unable to visit Asta's grave?

Like my grandmother, my mother never voluntarily talked about Asta. If I asked a question about her sister, Mom's answers were often abrupt and sometimes angry. Whenever she did mention her sister, the scattered stories my mother told provided only a partial picture of the person Asta once was.

Even though Mom told me little about Asta's life, I discovered that my mother, like my grandmother, preserved memorabilia that she considered too precious to discard. Among the fancy jewelry she kept in a box on her dressing table, Mom saved Asta's engagement ring, and I later found Asta's diary, nestled among the important family records my mother saved in a drawer next to her bed.

When my grandmother died, my mother retrieved Asta's black and white photograph, the one that had once been so prominently displayed in my grandmother's apartment. From its new location in my mother's bedroom, Asta's smiling face greeted my mother every morning and every evening when she got in and out of bed.

According to an old Estonian custom, women do not speak the names of those relatives who have died for three months after their deaths. After Asta died, my family chose to rarely mention her name, but it was clear that their memory of Asta was always with them, enshrined in the pictures and mementoes that they saved.

Throughout my childhood, Asta hovered like a dark shadow in the background of our family life. I could never know when a memory of Asta might silently drift across a family gathering. I wondered if a roaring fire at Christmas reminded my mother of holidays in Estonia when all the members of her family were still alive. Did a light summer breeze prompt Mom to recall happy summer days when she sunbathed with her sister at a nearby lake? Or did the smell of a hospital antiseptic take her back to the days when she sat next to her sister's hospital bed, hoping to see any signs of recovery?

The painful past that was part of my family history was a blank page that I struggled to fill. Since Estonia was a far-away and out-of-reach country that my relatives did not want to discuss, I found it difficult to picture what my mother's life was like while she was growing up. The trauma her family suffered during the war years was even harder for me to comprehend.

Yet, the traces of my family's history lingered in the sadness I could see in my mother's smile as the gloomy past lurked just behind our day-to-day reality. Even though my family's history was not discussed, I knew that the past had made an imprint on the way my mother approached her life. It also became the world view that affected how she raised me.

While Mom was stoic, pragmatic, and levelheaded, she learned as a young woman, how easily her world could be uprooted. Life, she discovered, could be cruel and unfair, leaving her displaced and exiled far from her homeland. Life, she also learned, could rip away the people she most loved. Her experiences taught her to anticipate the worst, since everything she had taken for granted had so easily disappeared. Moreover, her experiences from the war years left her questioning whether there was any true justice in the way crimes committed during the war were acknowledged, much less prosecuted.

How could the Western countries turn a blind eye, she asked, when the Soviet Union occupied much of Eastern Europe at the end of World War II? Why was it, she wanted to know, that the Allied countries prosecuted key Nazi leaders as war criminals, while the crimes committed by Joseph Stalin and other Soviet officials were overlooked? For many, Estonia, along with Latvia and Lithuania, were countries that few people in the United States could find on a map. Yet, from my mother's perspective, every sovereign country, no matter how small, should have the right to exist without fearing that it could be invaded by a larger more aggressive neighbor.

I grew up knowing about the injustice of Estonia's lost independence, but it was only when I traveled to Estonia with my mother when I was thirty-five, that the puzzle pieces from my family's Estonian history slowly began to come together. At the time of our trip in 1985, Estonia was still part of the Soviet Union. While I was discovering my mother's homeland for the first time, Mom was making her first trip back to Estonia after more than forty years.

Even though the two-week trip only gave me a sketchy picture of Estonia, my family was able to recover three photo albums, two of which belonged to Asta. Through the grainy photographs, I began to get a picture of the life my mother lived before the war. The albums also allowed me to begin seeing Asta for the person she once was.

Nearly twenty years later, I returned to Estonia in 2005 to visit my brother, Michael. After Estonia became independent in 1991, Michael moved to Tartu to work as a lawyer under contract with the U.S. Agency for International Development. Several years later, he decided to make Estonia his permanent home. With Michael as my guide, I visited Estonia with my husband and two children to try once again to connect with my Estonian heritage. During our trip, we visited Viljandi, my mother's hometown and toured the farm in rural Estonia where my grandfather had grown up.

Nearly three decades later, I travelled to Estonia once again in 2018 and with Michael's help, visited the Estonian National Archives where we were able to recover wartime documents that detailed the arrest of Bruno Kulgma Kull, Asta's fiancée. Among the over one hundred pages in Bruno's file, we discovered that Bruno, who was a lawyer, had submitted lengthy defense materials that answered many of my questions regarding why he was arrested and how he tried to defend himself.

My efforts to learn about my family's past have taken years, but over time, I have been able to piece together how my mother survived during the war and why Asta and Bruno were less fortunate. World War II disrupted the lives of hundreds of thousands of Estonians, who, like my mother and her family, would find new homes far from their Estonian homeland. They were able to avoid the fate of the many Estonians who were arrested, deported, executed, or killed during the war.

While my grandparents and my mother adapted to living in the United States, I sensed a void in the new lives they created for themselves. Part of their identity was missing, as they quietly mourned the loss of their homeland and lamented the friends and relatives they had left behind. Even while they committed themselves to living in the present, they also clung to the memory of Asta, whose death they could never accept and whose loss they never wanted to forget.

They were Estonians, but the country they knew had disappeared. After Estonia was subsumed within the Soviet Union, the nation's history became defined by the absence of what once was. This missing narrative also became part of my own life story, a part of who I was that I never fully understood while I was growing up.

When a photographer took Asta's black and white picture at the beginning of 1939, the war in Estonia had not yet begun. From what my mother told me, her sister was a 20-year-old medical student who dreamed about a future that she hoped to share with her fiancée, Bruno. Only six months after she posed for her picture, the Soviet army occupied Estonia and began installing military bases in strategic locations throughout the country. A year later, the Soviets orchestrated a rigged election and began taking control over Estonia's government, businesses, health care systems and schools.

To resist the Soviet take-over, Bruno, along with many other patriotic Estonians, tried to resist the Communist Party officials who were taking their orders from Moscow. They were brave, defiant, and willing to risk their lives to defend their country. They were also doomed to fail. For years, Bruno's story remained unknown to me. The details of his short life lay buried in an unmarked grave close to the spot where he was executed. Yet he left behind a legacy of patriotism and self-sacrifice, as well as a narrative that has become mine to tell.

Photo of Asta Vares, 1939, Viljandi, Estonia

CHAPTER 2

REMEMBERING ASTA

While Asta was an enigma to me throughout most of my life, a patchwork of clues began emerging to fill in the blurry contours of the person Asta had been. I also came to understand why Asta was so beloved. My mother revered Asta, but as I listened to her stories, I realized that as a younger sister, Mom felt as if she was always in Asta's shadow.

One afternoon, when I commented on the many three-inch high heel shoes my mother stored in her closet, she admitted, "I always wanted to be tall like Asta. When my mother tried to get me to wear Asta's hand-me-down clothes, they never quite fit. Asta was always taller and thinner – the way I wanted to be."

In my mind, Asta started to take shape as a slender young woman who stood a head taller than my mother. From her pictures, I could see that she was attractive, with an intelligent, inquisitive way of looking at the world, but rather than call attention to herself, she chose to wear her hair in a short, no-nonsense bob, and preferred sensible shoes.

Our family's Estonian albums show that as young children, Asta and my mother often wore identical clothes and identical smiles. Their affection for one another was obvious, as they stood side by side and laughed at their own inside jokes.

My mother recalled they were always together.

"While my parents worked in Dad's office, Asta and I spent our days with my grandmother, Tatsu. We lived in our own little world. I always followed Asta wherever she went."

Even though the two sisters dressed alike and spent much of their early lives together, Mom conceded they were different from one another. While Asta was a serious student who earned perfect grades, my mother admitted that her own academic performance did not equal her sister's stellar performance.

Years later, Mom still recalled my grandfather's dismay when she brought home her report cards.

"My poor father shook his head when he looked at my grades and would always tell me that I should try harder," she said wistfully.

On another occasion, Mom remembered how the family's piano teacher often compared the two sisters. After Asta played a piano piece without any seeming effort, the teacher rapped on my mother's knuckles and told her she needed to spend more time practicing. Surely, if Asta could master the hardest piano compositions, the teacher remained convinced that my mother should be able to match her sister's accomplishments.

Mom recalled that beyond being a serious student and an accomplished piano player, Asta was dedicated to becoming a physician. Even though both Asta and my mother chose to study medicine when they enrolled at the University of Tartu, Mom admitted that she only selected medicine as a major because she was even less interested in law or engineering, which were her other two options.

Thinking about what might have been, Mom said, "Asta would have been a wonderful doctor. Medicine was her passion and she really cared about other people. She was so much like my father, generous, kind-hearted, and always thinking about how to make the world a better place."

Photos from the family album confirm that Asta was a serious student, often capturing her bent over her schoolbooks. Yet, the pictures also reveal that Asta could be warmhearted and affectionate. Her life seemed to revolve around other people, as she huddled in the snow next to her classmates or hugged her young cousins during a summer vacation at the family farm.

She can be seen walking arm in arm with her closest girlfriends and in another photo, she posed next to my grandfather with her hand on his shoulder. When she gathered with large groups of friends, I noticed that Asta typically looked at those around her rather than staring at the photographer who was snapping the pictures.

My search through the family albums also revealed that Asta had an adventuresome and mischievous side to her personality. In one photo, standing in a tomboy pose, she proudly displayed a large plaster bandage on her knee. In another shot, she playfully splashed water on my mother's back at a lakeside resort. Her life, as revealed by her albums, was filled with fun adventures as she picnicked with large groups of friends and enjoyed cross-country ski trips during the winter.

In the carefree years before the start of World War II, Asta saved pictures of the New Year's Eve parties and formal balls that she enjoyed with her friends. She appeared happy, carefree, and surrounded by the many people she loved. Within the pages of her album, she included the class photos of more than forty young men and women, many of whom wrote affectionate notes.

"Everyone wanted to be Asta's friend," my mother would often say.

Even though Mom and her sister were two years apart in age, Asta made sure that my mother was invited to be a part of the many parties and social events she planned.

"Asta always invited me to join her buddies, especially if they were going to do something fun," Mom explained. "It made me feel so grown up when she asked me to be a part of her group."

As their daily lives became so closely intertwined, the devotion between the sisters deepened. Mom remembered, "Asta was a better person than I ever was. She was the best friend anyone could have, always listening to others without judgment and connecting with people in a way I never could. She was kind, forgiving, and compassionate and I adored her."

During the 1920s, while Asta and my mother were growing up, Estonia was a newly independent country that gained its freedom from the Soviet Union after a hard-fought War of Independence. Unlike my grandfather and grandmother, who came of age while Estonia was still part of Tsarist Russia, the two sisters only knew Estonia as a sovereign country whose citizens were defiantly independent, fiercely patriotic, and strongly protective of their country's right to exist.

The pictures in Asta's album freeze moments from the 1930s when most Estonians believed their lives would always be secure and predictable. While Asta dreamed of dedicating herself to caring for her patients as a physician, my mother must have imagined a future life centered around her family's home in Viljandi where her sister would always be by her side.

"Asta was just always there. We shared a bedroom and knew everything about each other's lives. When I needed a friend, she was the one who listened to me. I didn't realize how much I relied on her until she was gone," Mom recalled.

The close affinity between the two sisters can be seen in the idyllic photo taken in 1937, that shows Asta and my mother picking apples. As they basked in the summer sun, Mom stared directly at the camera with a confident smile, while Asta stood on the next rung of the ladder with her arm on my mother's shoulder as she studied something that she held in her other hand.

My mother with her sister, Asta, Viljandi, 1937

During one Christmas while I was visiting for the holidays, Mom became reflective as she remembered an occasion when the two sisters tried to predict their futures. Following an old Estonian superstition, Anna, the family maid, had convinced the girls to use lead- pouring to learn what the upcoming year might bring.

After Anna encouraged the sisters to sit around the kitchen table, she melted small pieces of lead on the stove while she gathered a bucket of snow from outside the kitchen door. Once everything was set, Asta leaned forward to gather a spoonful of lead and then threw the lead into the bucket that was filled with snow. Mom said when Anna recovered the hardened pieces of lead, they looked like misshapen lumps of metal. Yet Anna declared that Asta was going to be lucky because one of the shapes resembled an angel, a sign that over the next year she would find true love.

To make sure her lead fragment was better than Asta's, my mother filled the ladle with an extra portion of lead and threw it into the cold water with a strong flick of her wrist. But instead of taking shape, the lead scattered into five separate balls. When Anna laughed and announced that the pieces of hardened lead meant my mother was destined to have five children, Mom insisted this future scenario could not possibly be true. Anna and Asta merely smiled.

Recalling the story decades later, my mother became pensive. Even though she refused to believe the prediction, she did indeed have five children, a fate far different from what she planned for herself. Asta's prediction also came true. Before she died, Mom said her sister did find true love.

As the two girls pondered their future on that snowy December night, neither could have imagined that within a few years a war would come to Estonia and totally upend their lives. Nor could the two girls have accepted that Asta had only five more years to live.

Mom admitted that she could never imagine a time when her sister would not be nearby.

"After my sister died, I would often think—there's something I should tell Asta or I'd wonder what Asta would think about this or that situation. I could not wrap my mind around the fact that I could no longer reach out and talk with her. I refused to accept that Asta would never again be a part of my life. Even thinking about Asta made me want to cry, so I had to put her memory aside."

Mom was stubborn, single-minded, and tenacious in her will to survive, particularly after she was forced to learn a new language and create a life for herself in the United States. While my mother taught me to be self-reliant, I realized that I often relied on her the way she relied on her sister. I never wanted to accept a time when this strong-willed woman was not a part of my life.

On the morning when my father called to tell me that Mom had been hospitalized, I fooled myself into believing that she could not be seriously ill. Even though years earlier her doctors had discovered an aneurysm at the base of her brain, aside from some occasional dizzy spells, my mother's health condition did not interfere with her life. But, when she woke up one night with a splitting headache, my father, who was a physician, recognized that she needed immediate medical attention and called for an ambulance.

After the neurosurgeons determined that Mom's aneurysm had ruptured, they assured Dad that they could insert a stent to bypass the burst artery. The subsequent surgery was successful, but Mom suffered a stroke during the operation. Over the next few months, she recovered her ability to walk and talk, but the person she once was had disappeared, along with her memories from the past.

During my last visit with my mother, six months before she died at the age of ninety-two, we sat together at her kitchen table, sipping our coffee. Frail and confused, Mom was trying to make sense of the morning headlines, when she suddenly glanced up and looked at me with a puzzled expression. She recognized that I was someone familiar, but through the foggy depths of her memory, she could not quite place me.

Seeing her bewildered look, I asked, "Mom, do you know who I am?"

"Yes. You're my good friend, Rosalie," she said.

Dismayed that my mother no longer recognized me, I gently explained, "No. Mom, I'm Kaia, your oldest daughter."

Mom frowned, as she tried to make sense of how she could have a daughter that she no longer remembered and then looked down at the newspaper to hide her confusion.

Minutes later she abruptly asked, "Can you tell me why she had to die?"

Knowing she was referring to Asta, I said, "No one can know why things happen, Mom. It's just life."

Since my mother's stroke had erased much of her memory, I was astonished that decades after Asta's death, Mom was still questioning why her sister had passed away. Even though my mother had forgotten most of the details regarding her life, she never forgot the sister she lost.

Once again, the ghostly image of the slender young woman my mother adored drifted into view. I found myself wondering whether Asta could have survived if the history of World War II in Estonia had been different. What would have been the course of her life if her fiancée, Bruno, had not been arrested?

Any number of possible scenarios might have occurred, yet the tragic circumstances of World War II disrupted the lives of tens of thousands of Estonians. By the end of the war, one in four Estonians would be gone from the country. [2] Some died during the war while others were deported. Estonian refugees, like my mother and her family, ended up in Sweden, Canada, the United Kingdom, Australia, and the United States, choosing to escape rather than to live under the Soviets when they took control of Estonia at the end of the war.

The choice to become a stateless refugee is never an easy one to make. Yet, during our family trip to Estonia in 1985, I discovered how much more challenging my mother's life would have been if she had not been able to leave.

---

2   "Estonia in World War II," Wikipedia.

CHAPTER 3

WHAT MIGHT HAVE BEEN

When my mother had her first opportunity to return to Estonia at the age of sixty-three, more than forty years had gone by since the end of World War II. Even though she had spent four decades away from her homeland, Mom still considered herself to be Estonian. Yet, her identity was connected to an Estonia that ceased to exist after the Soviet Union absorbed the country into the U.S.S.R.

In the mid-1980s, when the Soviets first opened travel to the Baltic countries in a quest for Western dollars, Mom decided to travel back to her homeland and invited my brothers, Jim and Michael, my sister Tina, and me to come along. She was ambivalent about the trip. Although she wanted to reconnect with her past, Mom was wary of what she might find after the Soviets had spent decades trying to erase the country's independent past.

I, too, was unsure of what might remain of the country Mom and her family had left so many years earlier. For me, Estonia was a place on the map, close to Finland and Sweden, but located within the solid red block that designated the borders of the Soviet Union. Even though I recognized our trip would be an opportunity to experience Estonia as a country with its own unique sights and sounds, the restrictions the Soviets imposed on our travel plans led me to question how much of my family's past I might be able to discover.

Working with a Soviet-sponsored travel agency, Mom made the arrangements for our family group to fly to Finland and then take a ferry to Tallinn, Estonia's capital. After she booked rooms in a hotel that was designated for Western travelers, she also reserved a Soviet-approved guide to escort us during the day trip we planned to take to my mother's hometown of Viljandi, since the Soviets restricted any overnight travel outside of the capital city.

While we were on board the ferry that carried us from Helsinki to Tallinn, Mom became introspective and absorbed in her mixed feelings about returning to her home country. Reconnecting with Estonia would allow her to remember her happy memories of being a young girl surrounded by her family and friends. But the return trip also meant that she would relive the desperation and fear she felt during the war years.

As the Helsinki ferry docked, I thought about the historical accounts that described the chaotic scene in Tallinn harbor when the Soviet troops were rapidly advancing toward the capitol city. Black smoke shrouded the seaport after the German army set large tanks of oil on fire. While panicked Estonians rushed to join the Germans as they retreated, German soldiers hurried to fill the awaiting transport ships with their evacuating troops, wounded soldiers, and military equipment.

When the Nazi soldiers tried to clear the gangplanks, mobs of Estonians rushed forward in their effort to try to board the ships. Everyone knew that the Soviet army was less than a day away from occupying Estonia's capital city and there were few escape routes. After the German sailors were finally able to pull up the anchors, disengage the dock lines, and prepare the transport ships to depart, the Estonians who had boarded the ships sang the Estonian national anthem while the throngs of refugees who had been left behind cried out in despair.

In contrast with that frantic scene, the Tallinn harbor my family discovered in 1985 was a peaceful, out-of-the way seaport where a century's old past lived next to a more futuristic present. Largely untouched during World War II, Tallinn's old town center retained its medieval stone walls, red-tiled roofs, and cobblestone streets. Yet, the city center with its gothic church steeples and castle-like fortifications was surrounded by stark Soviet-style buildings.

Not far from Tallinn harbor, we arrived at the Hotel Viru, a twenty-story, glass-fronted structure that the Soviets had commissioned to have built for Western visitors. While we were registering with the hotel clerk, an elderly woman hobbled toward us and grabbed my mother by the arm. I noticed she was missing most of her teeth and wore her wizened grey hair in a tight bun.

"Don't you remember me?" she said. "I'm Liina."

Mom stared at first and then recognized her former classmate.

"Liina, what brings you here?"

Breathing heavily, Liina looked at each of us, and said, "I've been waiting in the lobby for the past week when I heard you were coming back."

As a tear rolled down her cheek, her voice trembled.

Turning to us, Mom explained, "Liina and I were bench mates. We sat next to each other in grammar school. She was always the better student."

Liina blushed and shook her head, "Now your mother is making things up. Do you have time to talk?"

Nodding, Mom guided her friend towards the hotel lounge that was filled with garish green leather couches and low pole lamps. While my mother wore a stylish red tailored jacket, her school pal limped next to her in a worn, bulky coat and a full-length skirt. As we were finding our seats, Liina looked over her shoulder at the front desk clerk who kept a watchful eye on our small group.

After we sat down, Liina began speaking in a hushed whisper, leaning forward to make sure my mother could hear what she was saying. As her anguished words spilled out in a torrent of Estonian, my mother sat grimly beside her friend and nodded her head. Even though Mom did her best to translate for us, we captured only fragments of the larger story Liina wanted to share.

From time to time, when Mom asked a question, Liina launched into another whispered tirade, shaking her head, and punctuating her sentences with the tip of her finger. On the occasions when my mother's former classmate paused to catch her breath, Mom stopped to share the gist of what Liina was telling her.

She is explaining what happened to some of the people we knew.

One of them was deported to Siberia. Liina had to go as well.

After she returned, she got married and had a child, but the Soviets sent her back.

She is telling me how many of our friends have died.

She is telling me about her health problems.

We sat in somber silence while Liina continued her stories about what happened after the war and how life in Estonia had changed. Finally, when there was no more to say, she got up, gave my mother a brief hug, and then stood in front of each of us as she shook our hands. When she was done saying good-bye, we watched as she limped toward the lobby door.

Overwhelmed, Mom could only say, "It's a good thing we got on that boat."

Liina and her family were among the ten thousand Estonians who were deported by the Soviets in 1941 during the first deportation the Soviets orchestrated in the Baltic states.[3] Although she was able to return to Estonia after the war, she was arrested once again and sent back to Siberia as part of the second mass deportation of Estonian citizens that the Soviets conducted on March 25, 1949. Her sad story was one shared by many Estonians.

After Liina said goodbye, we took an elevator to our hotel rooms. When we reached our floor, we noticed an older Russian woman sitting in a folding chair with a notebook in her lap. As she watched us walk down the hallway, her intense stare made us feel uncomfortable. While Mom chose to ignore her, my brothers started ribbing each other, whispering, and then glancing back.

---

3   *Estonian World*, "Estonia Remembers the Soviet Deportations."

The next morning at breakfast we laughed as Michael and Jim shared how they pretended to be spies when they were back in their room. Jokingly, they made up stories as they asked each other how many military planes they counted at the airport and whether they had captured pictures of the army tanks near the runways. Even though they did not believe their room was bugged, they spoke loudly into the lamps and questioned whether there could be a microphone hidden inside.

As Americans, we found it preposterous to think we were under surveillance, yet as we came to understand, this was very much a fact of life for many Estonians. The cousin who came to pick us up for a family gathering later that afternoon was detained several hours for questioning.

When Estonia regained its independence seven years after our trip, the new hotel managers did indeed uncover a Soviet KGB radio center on the twenty-third floor of the Hotel Viru. They discovered listening devices in the hotel walls, in phones, and even in flowerpots. The Soviets had also hidden microphones in ashtrays and on the bottom of bread plates. My brothers may have joked about being spies, but the Soviet agents who were monitoring the hotel most likely considered their conversation to be highly suspicious.

After we completed our breakfast, we set out with our Soviet-approved driver to travel to Viljandi. Mom only told us we would be having lunch with my grandmother's cousin, a man named Enno, along with his family. Driving south from Tallinn, we passed by acres of wide-open fields that were interrupted from time to time by groves of trees and collections of farmhouses. The expansive landscape was sparse and largely unsettled. Self-conscious that the driver could hear our conversation, we sat in silence, tightly packed next to one another for the two-hour drive.

Viljandi, we discovered, was a small town nestled along a meandering lake. As we drove along the narrow, cobblestone streets, we passed a mixture of wood-framed houses, two-story office buildings, and tree-lined parks. Near the center of town, Mom pointed out the white stucco town hall where my grandfather once served as Mayor. She also showed us the red brick café where she remembered that my grandmother liked to have coffee with her friends.

While Mom rediscovered some of the buildings that she recalled from her childhood, she noticed that other structures had disappeared. In the middle of an open park, Mom told us there was once a large granite statue that commemorated the Estonian War of Independence.

"The Soviets," she said, "Blew it up at the beginning of the war."

What else was missing? I wondered.

Following Mom's directions, the driver parked in front of a large, two-story, stucco house located on the corner of a shady parkway, a short walking distance from the town square. My mother told us it had once been her family's home, as well as the site where my grandfather, Jaan Vares, had his medical office. During our 1985 visit, we could not go into the house because the Soviet authorities had converted the building into a childcare facility.

"Besides," Mom said, "There was nothing to see, and we are already late for lunch."

Around the corner from the house, we found Enno, a short, stooped man with bushy, grey hair, who was waiting for us in his front yard when our car pulled up. He cried when he hugged my mother, saying he never thought he would see her again in this lifetime.

After being escorted into his home, we were introduced to Enno's two daughters, their husbands, and children, as well as a family friend who would be joining us for lunch. To accommodate our large group, Enno's wife Nina replaced the furniture in the family's living room with a long table where we sat for our meal.

During our lunch, we asked Enno where he had been at the end of the war. He explained that he was returning home after maneuvers with the German army when he found an urgent message from my mother, telling him he should join the family since the German transport ships were about to leave. Hoping to reach the harbor, Enno jumped on a bicycle, but shortly after leaving Viljandi, he heard the rumbling of nearby Russian tanks. To avoid being captured, he stripped off his German army uniform and returned to town in civilian clothes.

I later learned that after the war Enno was one of my grandmother's most faithful correspondents. During the Soviet occupation, he wrote updates to my grandmother to assure her that he was caring for her mother, Tatsu. When he decided to relocate from the Vares family home to the house next door, he salvaged several household items that he then shipped to my grandmother, including a multi-colored rug that she had handloomed during happier times.

On the afternoon of our visit, Enno proudly presented my mother with three family albums that he had been saving for more than forty years. Two had been compiled by Asta while another contained the photos my mother collected while she was a senior in high school and a freshman in college. Even though Enno could not have known whether my mother would ever come to retrieve the albums, he believed it was his duty to preserve this record of the family who had been such an important part of his life after his mother died. Mom was grateful to recover the albums and presented Enno with the gifts she brought for his family, including several pairs of blue jeans that were coveted in Estonia during that time.

Before we left Viljandi, Mom explained that we would be taking a short car ride. After she informed our Soviet driver where we were going, we travelled with Enno to a nearby cemetery. Without having been told, my siblings and I knew we would be visiting Asta's grave.

Walking up a steep gravel path, we came upon a narrow grave site set on the side of a hill overlooking Viljandi. Holding my mother's hand, Enno explained that he planted flowers on Asta's grave every year and lit a candle on Christmas Eve to make sure she would always be remembered.

None of us knew what to say. Only Enno and my mother remembered Asta as a beloved family member. Around us, the heavily wooded cemetery was divided into a maze of family plots separated by fences, shrubbery, and benches. We found ourselves surrounded by pedestals and granite gravestones that marked the successive passing of generations of Estonian families. By comparison, Asta's grave seemed isolated and lonely. Her single burial plot stood removed from the far away cemeteries where other members of her family were buried. While her tombstone offered the simple facts of her abbreviated life, the story of the person she once was continued to be a mystery to me.

Asta's gravesite in Viljandi

CHAPTER 4

RECOVERING THE PAST

When my family visited Estonia in the summer of 1985, no one could have predicted that just five years later, Estonia, Latvia, and Lithuania would declare their independence from the U.S.S.R. Since the Soviets had occupied the Baltic countries and much of Eastern Europe for nearly fifty years, the prospect that the Soviet Union could dissolve was a dream few expected to come true.

During the five decades when Estonia was occupied by the Soviet Union, much of the country's wartime history was rewritten to fit a Soviet narrative, one that our Soviet-approved tour guide explained during our 1985 visit to Tallinn.

"All Estonians," she said, "should be grateful to the heroic Soviet soldiers who fought against the German Nazis to free Estonia from fascism."

During the postwar Soviet occupation of Estonia, Estonian school children were taught a Soviet controlled version of their country's history, one in which Estonia's independent past was labelled a "bourgeois nationalism" that needed to be erased.[4] One Estonian writer described the Soviet efforts to reconstruct his country's history as a form of constant brainwashing that was designed to eliminate any evidence that Estonia had ever been independent.[5]

In response to pressure from the Baltic ex-patriot community, the U.S. Congress passed nearly one hundred resolutions during the decades after the war in which the American legislators demanded freedom for Estonia, Latvia, and Lithuania, but my mother was always cynical that any real change would occur.

"The Soviets will never let Estonia be free. Just you watch." she would frequently remind me.

Despite the iron grip the Soviets appeared to have over Estonia, protests organized in the late 1980s began pressuring the Soviet authorities to allow the country to regain its independence. During a gathering in Tallinn's old-town city center in June 1988, one hundred thousand Estonians sang outlawed patriotic songs as they waved the Estonian national flag. A few months later, more than three hundred thousand demonstrators rallied in Tallinn's songfest amphitheater where they called for Estonia to be free from Soviet control. Throughout Latvia and Lithuania, similar protests were also being organized.

During the fall months, the size of the protest movement crowds continued to grow. In response, the Soviets introduced changes to Estonia's constitution that prohibited Soviet republics from seceding from the U.S.S.R. Reacting to the

---

4   Estonian State Commission, "The White Book," 103

5   Estonian State Commission, "The White Book," 60.

constitutional change, nine hundred thousand Estonians signed a petition opposing the modifications the Soviets had introduced.

Empowered by the growing number of protestors, the Estonian parliament issued a proclamation that declared the Soviet occupation of Estonia to be illegal. The legislators also called for a transition period to allow Estonia to move towards becoming a sovereign state. As they tried to dampen the burgeoning move towards independence, the Soviets decided to allow Estonians to celebrate Christmas for the first time in nearly forty years.[6]

Back in the United States, Mom joined other Baltic protestors who organized marches in Philadelphia. She also donated to local activist groups, signed petitions, attended lectures, and on several occasions, provided lodging to visiting Estonian dignitaries. On the 50th anniversary of Estonia's first declaration of independence, she hosted a large gathering where her Estonian friends toasted the prospect that Estonia might one day become independent again.

Throughout the Baltics, the promise of freedom energized two million people from Estonia, Latvia, and Lithuania to come together on August 23, 1989. By joining their arms, they formed a continuous human chain that extended more than 420 miles. As they cheered and sang patriotic songs, men and women, retirees and housewives, grandparents and children joined their voices to demand independence for the Baltic states. In solidarity fellow demonstrators marched in

---

6   Kelam and Ahonen, "The Singing Revolution."

Berlin, Leningrad, Moscow, Melbourne, Stockholm, Tbilisi, and Toronto.[7]

Sparked by the strength of the protest movement, other resistance groups began forming throughout Eastern Europe. In Poland the Solidarity labor union, a flashpoint for dissent, was legally recognized while Hungarian protesters dismantled the 150 miles of barbed wire that separated their country from Austria.

In East Germany, Berliners took advantage of a decree intended to ease cross-border travel to tear down the Berlin Wall. As the iconic barrier that separated Berlin into two sectors came down, students in Prague clashed with police while dissenters in Romania overthrew the Communist dictator, Nicolae Ceausescu.

As the protests continued, Mikhail Gorbachev, the president of the Soviet Union, decided not to use the Soviet military to intervene. Acknowledging the resentment the Baltic states felt toward the Molotov-Ribbentrop Pact, he formed a commission that reviewed the diplomatic protocol and denounced the Pact on December 24, 1989.

Alarmed at the success the fledgling independence movements were having throughout Eastern Europe, Moscow hardliners placed President Gorbachev under house arrest on August 18, 1991, a move they said was necessary "to restore the honor and dignity of the Soviet man."[8]

Not willing to back down, the Estonian parliament convened an emergency session in which they formed a

---

7 The Baltic Way, 1989-2014, History.

8 "1991 Soviet Coup d'Etat Attempt," Wikipedia.

constitutional assembly to establish a new legal system for the country. The Soviets responded by ordering a column of Red Army tanks and troop carriers to advance toward Tallinn and to take control over the communication tower from which the country's television and radio programs were being broadcast.

Worried that the nation's television broadcasts could be interrupted, a handful of Estonian paramilitary troops barricaded the entrance to the communication tower and threatened to blow it up if the Soviet troops tried to take it over. After a tense day-long siege, the Soviet soldiers retreated when they learned the coup attempt against Gorbachev had failed.

Even though the coup against him had collapsed, Gorbachev resigned as president of the U.S.S.R. on August 24 and was replaced by Boris Yeltsin. Working in concert with the leaders of the Ukraine and Belarus, Yeltsin then dissolved the Soviet Union, hoping to reconstitute the Soviet republics.

In response, Moldova, Azerbaijan, and Kyrgyzstan asserted they were sovereign states, followed by Estonia, Latvia, and Lithuania. Over the next few months, the republics seeking independence would be joined by Tajikistan, Armenia, Turkmenistan, and Ukraine, all of whom chose to separate from the Soviet Union.

My mother believed it was a miracle when Soviet lawmakers officially recognized Estonia's independence on September 6. Because the Soviet control over Estonia had lasted for nearly a half-century, few believed the country would ever regain its independence. Over the five decades that had gone by since the end of World War II, my grandparents and many others from their generation had died. Most of the soldiers who fought in World War II were retirees, and the generation of children who were born after the war had grown up only knowing a world in which the Soviets dominated Eastern Europe.

Among the correspondence my mother saved, I found a letter in which Enno described the euphoria Estonians experienced when they could finally believe that their struggle for independence had been successful.

December 25, 1991

Greetings Little Family,

On this Christmas Day, I send you greetings from Viljandi and remember fondly when we were last together. So much has happened since you left, I can hardly believe it. I know you have heard the news about the fall of the Berlin Wall and the opening of Eastern Europe.

The drumbeat of freedom was also beating strong in Estonia during these days. I can't begin to explain how thrilling it was for me to be part of what people are now calling the Baltic Chain. Imagine two million people from the Baltic countries joining hands from Tallinn, through Latvia and all the way to Vilnius in Lithuania to protest the Molotov–Ribbentrop pact between Germany and Russia that allowed the Soviets to claim control of the Baltic countries so long ago. We held hands, sang the Estonian national anthem, and tried to show the world the tragedy of that historical injustice.

For fifty years we kept alive our dream of being independent and now that dream which seemed so far away for so long has become a reality. For the first time in the lives of my children, Estonia is finally once again independent. It was just this summer that the Soviets formally recognized Estonia as our own, free, and independent country and I hope it won't be long before the final Russian troops pack up and leave.

I'm so thankful the transition was peaceful. Yes, there was some intimidation by the Soviets, and the Russian troops seemed as if they were itching for a confrontation, but in the end our brave patriots stood steadfast in front of the Soviet tanks, and it worked. I never believed I would live to see this day. It's the dream of a lifetime.

So, on this Christmas Day, I send you greetings for the first time from a free Estonia and blessings for the New Year. We hope that this is a year that will bring you back for another visit.

Wishing you all the best.
Yours, Enno

Over the next year, our family watched and cheered as Estonia reestablished a parliamentary democracy with a freely elected prime minister and an independent judiciary. Under the newly established Constitution, all individuals were given the right to a fair trial and guaranteed access to legal counsel.

Those who were arrested for political crimes under the Soviet regime were released. Under the rules established by the newly constituted legal system, the Chief Justice of the Estonian Supreme Court, Rait Maruste, disregarded the death penalty orders that remained on his desk from the Soviet era.

While largely symbolic, Estonian prosecutors began war crime trials to reverse the decades-long imposition of a Soviet code of law that dictated who was innocent and who was guilty as defined by the U.S.S.R legal system. While the Estonian courts were seeking justice for Soviet-era crimes, the Estonian parliament moved to restore the ownership rights to those whose property was appropriated during the two Soviet occupations. Under these new legal provisions, my mother's brother, Jaan, was able to reclaim ownership of the Vares family home.

As the legal reforms were under way in Estonia, my brother, Michael, who was working as an attorney in Philadelphia, signed up to be a legal consultant under a program established by the U.S. Agency for International Development. After Michael moved to Tartu in 1994, he became part of a legal cadre that assisted Estonia's legal institutions in their transition from a Soviet to a Western system of law. As part of his work, Michael helped to create a legal education center (the Eesti Õiguskeskus), where he remained as a consultant for several more years. As his personal and professional connections in Estonia deepened, my brother decided to settle permanently in Tartu where he continues to live.

Excited to learn more about the independent country Estonia had become, I returned in 2005 with my husband and two teenage children. Compared with my first visit more than twenty years earlier, I discovered that my mother's homeland had become a flourishing country filled with restaurants, cafes, and shops offering Estonian souvenirs and crafts. As part of Estonia's renaissance, Tallinn had been transformed into a popular cruise ship destination where thousands of tourists disembarked throughout the summer season to tour the city's medieval center.

During our visit to Viljandi, my family was pleased to discover the town was hosting its Annual Folk Festival. As we walked toward the Castle Ruins Park, we found ourselves surrounded by throngs of international tourists who streamed through the cobblestone streets carrying backpacks and guitar cases. My grandfather would have been impressed by the crowds who made their way to the performance venues on the outskirts of town as they crossed over the Vares Bridge that he had, long ago, arranged to have constructed, when he was Viljandi's Mayor.

With Michael's help, we travelled to the village of Paistu to visit Sova, the farm that my grandfather's family had owned before the war. The Estonian countryside was bucolic, with sleepy hillsides where cattle grazed next to fields of alfalfa and rye. The dirt roads were dusty and since there were few signs, we made several wrong turns before finding the country lane that led to the site where the Vares family had lived for hundreds of years.

Based on the available written records I was able to review, I discovered that generations of my Estonian ancestors had lived in the Paistu region dating from the 17th century. Our family's connection to this land most likely extended back even further since, prior to being emancipated in 1816, Estonian serfs were not able to travel away from their local communities. They remained in place for centuries growing the crops that enabled them to survive while they endured outbreaks of plague, years of famine, and the havoc caused by warring armies.

At the end of the 19th century, my great-grandfather, Jaan Vares, was proud when he became the first in his family to own his farm instead of leasing it from the local German manor lord. He then doubled his acreage after he married Ann Jaanson who lived on a neighboring property. By the time he died in 1916 at the age of 58, Jaan had spent a lifetime toiling in his fields, as he worked to create an enduring heritage for his family and for those who were still to come.

Three decades after my great-grandfather's death, the Soviet Union imposed its post-war occupation on Estonia and forced my great-grandmother, Ann, to leave the family farm after it was appropriated into a local collective in the late 1940s. When one of my grandfather's relatives regained possession of the property after Estonia became independent, she sold it to some Finnish investors. At the time when my family visited the site in 2018, we found it to be uninhabited, desolate, and forlorn.

Knee-high weeds filled the courtyard in front of the family's two-story house where the windows and doors were boarded shut. To one side, we noticed a run-down barn with a sloping roof that was in obvious need of repair. Other than the sound of chirping crickets, there were no signs of life.

Twenty yards from the house, we found the oak tree that my great-grandmother, Ann, had planted on the spot where my great-grandfather lost his life in a farming accident. After nearly one hundred years, the tree towered over the field, but its white skeletal frame was barren. The oak had died, leaving behind only a stark shadow of the solid tree that once spread its limbs over the field. By the time we visited, it had become a lonely sentinel, standing guard over a vacant farmhouse and a wide swath of fallow fields.

What trace remained in my own life from the attachment my Estonian relatives once placed in the farmland they owned and cultivated? Along with other members of my immediate family, my home was thousands of miles from these fields that my great-grandfather had at one time nurtured. Moreover, my connection to my Estonian heritage had been largely severed while I was growing up since the Soviets prohibited travel in and out of the Baltic countries. Questions about my connection to my family's past continued to haunt me.

Over the next ten years, I researched my mother's ancestral tree and scanned through the black-and-white family albums from the prewar years. I searched through historical accounts from World War II and learned about the key events that occurred in Estonia during the war. I also charted the timeline of my family's escape and combed through memoirs and narrative histories written by Estonian authors.

After my mother died, I sorted through the documents she had saved and discovered a well-worn, palm-sized diary that intrigued me. My mother was not one to write letters nor did she ever scribble down her thoughts. Moreover, the handwriting on the dozen or more pages was unfamiliar.

After Michael helped me to have the Estonian text translated, I realized the small notebook could only have belonged to Asta. The entries started at the beginning of the Soviet occupation in 1939 and ended in 1941, when the Germans took control over Estonia. Through her writing, I was able to hear Asta's voice and connect more directly to her thoughts about the war that was taking place around her.

I discovered more information about what happened in Estonia during World War II when Michael and I visited the library housed at the Estonian National Museum. When I asked about reference materials dating from the war, a librarian pointed out the three-volume compendium that had been created by the Estonian International Commission for the Investigation of Crimes against Humanity. Through its work, the Commission investigated three periods of time: the initial Soviet occupation of Estonia, the German occupation, and the postwar occupation of Estonia by the Soviet Union.

As part of my search to understand Estonia's wartime experiences, Michael and I also made an appointment to visit the Estonian National Archives where we planned to review a thick folder filled with documents that detailed Bruno's arrest and imprisonment in the summer of 1941 through the spring of 1942. It was a crisp October morning when we made our way to the branch office of the Archives in Tallinn. We found the narrow entrance to the unremarkable building on a heavily wooded side street just beyond the center of town. Behind the nondescript front door, it was hard to believe that the Archives maintained a vast storage system containing millions of records, photos, films, and maps related to Estonian history.

At the time of our appointment, the translator Michael had hired joined us and together we settled around a thin, metal worktable near several other researchers who huddled over stacks of files at nearby tables. Anticipating our arrival, an archivist brought out a thick bundle of folders for us to review.

While we scanned through the papers within Bruno's file, we found police memos, interview summaries, and official documents that detailed Bruno's arrest and his subsequent transfer to a prison in Tartu. There were also letters of support, including one from my grandfather, as well as several official memos that were written in German.

Among the voluminous material, we were excited to discover a twenty-five-page, type-written testimony in which Bruno detailed his motivations for joining the Communist Party and his subsequent efforts to undermine the Party's efforts to usurp Estonia's independence. In addition, we found a thirteen-page, handwritten report in which Bruno described the inner workings of the Communist Party in Viljandi. Several other folders contained the expert testimony Bruno provided to protect a half dozen Estonians against charges that they were members of the Communist Party.

After wondering about Bruno's fate for years, I was eager to understand why he was arrested and convicted. Even though Michael and I were impatient to read the material, we needed to wait several weeks for the archivist to scan the extensive files. Once we received a digital copy of the material from Bruno's folder, Michael then arranged for an Estonian translator to convert the text into English. It would be a month after I returned from Estonia before Bruno's story finally began to emerge.

CHAPTER 5

THE HOUSE MY GRANDFATHER BUILT

More than thirty years after my first trip to Estonia, I was finally able to visit the inside of my mother's family home in Viljandi in 2018. At the time of my family's first trip to Estonia in 1985, the house had been off limits to visitors while the building was being used as a daycare center. After my Uncle Jaan regained ownership of the large, two-story, stucco building in the early 1990s, he allowed the operators of the daycare facility to continue using the space while he set up an apartment on the first floor where he could stay during his annual trips back to Estonia. More than a decade later, my uncle sold the large property to a developer who converted the space into apartments that were then bought by eight independent owners.

Nearly eighty years after World War II had ended, I tried to reimagine what the building might have been like in the prewar years when it was my mother's home, as well as the site where my grandfather maintained his medical office.

Pictures from the family album show that my grandfather placed a metal sign at the building's entrance where he advertised his services in internal medicine and dentistry. In the front section of the first floor, he set up a reception area, several exam rooms, as well as a dental clinic and a separate space for his X-ray equipment.

Toward the back of the house, the Vares family used the spacious rooms on the first floor for their living quarters. Behind the living room and dining area, they could watch through the paneled windows in their kitchen as the apple trees my grandfather planted in their ample backyard changed from season to season.

Before the war, my grandmother's parents, Tatsu and Eduard, occupied an apartment on the second floor along with Enno who came to live with Tatsu (his aunt) after his mother died. Down the hall, Bruno, Asta's fiancée, rented another unit with his widowed mother. During the 1940s, while they were in high school, both Bruno and Enno attended the Viljandi County Boy's High School where Enno was two grades ahead of Bruno.

The Vares family home in Viljandi, Estonia

My mother was proud that her father was well-known and respected in Viljandi because of his many contributions as a civic leader and community volunteer. As the oldest son, he was in line to inherit his family farm in Paistu, but he chose instead to travel to Moscow to study medicine.

After returning to Estonia in 1919, he built a thriving medical practice while also staying active in Viljandi's local government. Between 1925 through 1929, he was the Mayor of Viljandi and then continued to serve on the town council for nearly twenty years. He also headed the local chapter of the Red Cross, stayed active in numerous Estonian cultural associations, and served as a board member for several education and commercial organizations.

When my grandfather turned fifty in January of 1939, the Viljandi town leaders honored his many civic contributions by organizing a choral concert. In the newspaper story that described the celebration, my grandfather was characterized as a fatherly figure who was beloved for his commitment to his patients and for his contributions to the welfare of his town. The newspaper account concluded by summarizing the attributes that made my grandfather so revered.

> It is clear that no man can stand unopposed when they are consistently active in such a range of public areas. (Jaan Vares) is no stranger to having opponents and may well have more in the future, but he has never had and nor will ever have enemies. The jubilarian cannot have enemies for the simple reason that he himself does not consider anyone to be his enemy. Someone with a mind

as straightforward as Vares does not bear a grudge and in return no man can bear a grudge against him.[9]

Only five years after celebrating his fiftieth birthday, my grandfather was forced to leave behind his lifetime of accomplishments, his well-earned reputation as a physician and community activist, and his very identity as an Estonian. He was stoic about what he lost. Rather than complain, he focused on making the best of the circumstances in which he found himself.

During our 1985 visit to Estonia, when my mother returned to her hometown for the first time, she must have been reminded of all that her family had left behind when they escaped, since they carried only those items that would fit in their traveling trunks. During our afternoon meal with Enno, as she looked out towards her family home, she must have remembered the happier times when her family gathered to celebrate holidays and to share vacations. Both Enno and my mother would also have been painfully aware of the missing loved ones who were once so much a part of their lives, as the shadowy presence of Asta and Bruno drifted through their memories from the past.

---

9   *Viljandi Uudiseid,* "Dr. Jaan Vares 50."

*Asta stands in front of a window at the Vares family house
with my mother, Enno and a family
friend looking on from above.*

During our visit, Enno explained that he never lived far
from the Vares family home after the war. When the Soviet
army took control over Estonia in the fall of 1944, Enno
returned to the second-floor apartment he shared with Tatsu
and continued living with her until she died in the early 1950s.
When the apartment grew too small for his growing family,
Enno moved with his wife and two daughters to the house
next door where he was still living at the time of our visit in
1985.

On the warm summer day as we gathered in Enno's living
room, the building that was once the Vares family home
was quiet with no signs of life. The windows were dark, and
the doors were locked. Decades later, when Michael and I

reconnected with Enno's daughter, she arranged for us to meet Anna, one of the apartment owners who in turn offered to give us a tour of the eight units since all the other occupants were away for the weekend.

From what we could see, my grandfather's former home appeared to be in good hands. The building owners had replaced the roof and updated the windows. Towards the back of the house, I noticed neatly stacked cords of split wood while the basement walls were covered with floor-to-ceiling shelving that overflowed with canned fruits and vegetables.

Within each of the apartments, the living space was comfortably occupied with well-stocked kitchens, cozy sitting rooms, and scattered toys. Anna explained that when the apartment owners found a metal sign in the attic that read "Jaan Vares, Internal Medicine and Dentistry," they hung it in the foyer to honor my grandfather and to acknowledge the building's history.

Even though the renovated apartments had new occupants with their own life stories, I looked for the faint traces that this was the place where my mother and her family once lived before the war changed their lives. As Michael and I toured the second-floor apartments, I tried to imagine Bruno looking out through the back windows, as a hopeful law student and then later while he worried over when he was going to be arrested. I thought about the sound that his footsteps would have made as he climbed down the back stairs to spend time with Asta. Once he was arrested, I wondered how often Asta came up to his empty apartment to console herself as she waited for his release.

At the conclusion of our tour, Anna invited us to join her at her kitchen table where she wanted to know more about my grandfather and how our family escaped. Michael explained that the Vares family was able to leave Estonia on the last day before the Soviets arrived in the fall of 1944. We also told her about our visit to the Estonian National Archives where we had found additional information regarding Bruno's arrest.

Shaking her head, Anna said, "Every Estonian family has a story to tell."

Then she got up from the table and walked to a nearby bookshelf where she pulled down a thick volume that her great-aunt had arranged to have published. The text consisted of letters that were written after members of Anna's family were deported to Siberia. In the final letter, Anna's grandmother beseeched her sister to retrieve her two young daughters, one of whom was Anna's mother. Tears pooled in Anna's eyes as she read the final note in which her grandmother begged to be forgiven before she committed suicide. Generations later, the tragic loss of her grandmother still reverberated in Anna's life.

After our tour of the Vares family home, Michael and I arranged to meet with Heiki, a local historian who had written several books about Viljandi. As we settled into low leather chairs in the lobby of the Grand Hotel, we noticed that many of the visitors who passed by on their way to the hotel restaurant waved to Heiki who nodded in return. Viljandi, it appeared to us, was a place where everyone seemed to know one another.

After we explained the unanswered questions that we were seeking to explore, Heiki shared what he knew about our family's past.

"I know your father," he said, remembering a visit my parents had made to Viljandi twenty years earlier for Michael's wedding. Heiki also told us that he had written a book that described my grandfather's tenure while he was the Mayor of Viljandi. Then he added, "Your mother had a sister who died when she was very young. She was engaged to a Communist."

Michael and I were stunned. Bruno, we had been told, was a hero who joined the Communist Party to help the Estonian cause. How could he be remembered in Viljandi as a traitor? Perhaps it was true that Asta's fiancée was involved with the war crimes that occurred during the Soviet occupation.

Heiki went on to explain, "Life was messy during the war. Many Estonians were branded as either Communists or Fascists depending on whether they collaborated with the Soviets or the Germans."

Apparently, there was no middle road for those Estonians who wanted to promote Estonia's independence while the Soviets and then the Germans occupied the small Baltic nation. Heiki said that, after the war, the Soviets tried to erase any sign of Estonian nationalism while they worked to integrate the country within the Soviet Union.

"During the post-war Soviet occupation, much of the true story regarding those who tried to defend Estonia's independence was hidden from view."

Given the efforts that the Soviets had made to cover over Estonia's prewar history, I wondered what information might be available decades later that could help to explain whether Bruno was indeed a Communist traitor or a patriot who was trying to defend his homeland.

The task of putting together the puzzle pieces of my family's history seemed daunting. My brother and I had returned to the place where my mother and her family lived many years earlier, but it was difficult to comprehend what their lives had been like, particularly as they struggled during the war. Yet, I was optimistic that the material I had gathered from the Estonian National Archives would help to answer the many questions I had about my family's experiences while Estonia was occupied. I was also eager to unravel the mysteries that surrounded Bruno's arrest. Learning about my family's past became my full-time quest.

CHAPTER 6

FINDING BRUNO

Based on what I knew, Bruno seemed to be an unlikely traitor. Like many young people who grew up while Estonia was first establishing itself as a sovereign country, he was fiercely patriotic. As my mother explained, Estonia's quest for independence had deep roots. For generations, Estonians had preserved their own language and cultural identity despite a long history of occupation by Germany, Denmark, Sweden, Poland, and Russia.

After the country finally won its independence shortly after the Soviet Union was first formed, many Estonians had immense pride in their homeland.

"We were Estonians and proud of our small country. It was inconceivable to us that our freedom and identity as Estonians could be taken away," my mother said.

As a young schoolboy, Bruno would have joined his fellow classmates as he proudly waved the country's blue, black, and white flag when the veterans from Estonia's War of Independence were honored during the country's annual Independence Day celebrations. They were heroes who fought against all odds to enable Estonia to join the international community of nations. It was a sacrifice that Bruno also pledged to make when he sang lines from Estonia's national anthem,

"With my last breath my thanks to thee, for true to death I'll ever be,

O worthy, most beloved and fine, my dearest country mine!"

Available records show that Bruno was born on June 26, 1914. After his sister died, he became an only child. During his earliest years, he lived with his parents in a rural community in southern Estonia where his father, Mihkel, worked as a municipal secretary, a job to which Bruno would later aspire. Like other Estonian students, Bruno would have completed a school curriculum that included Estonian culture, history, and literature, a course of studies that nurtured his identity as an Estonian. He was a gifted student with a strong ambition to create a future for himself.

After Bruno's father died while he was in high school, Bruno took a series of odd jobs to support his widowed mother, working at the nearby mills, laboring as a farmhand, and performing clerical tasks. Forced at an early age to be resourceful, he became determined to earn enough money to put himself through college where his goal was to earn a law degree.

Even though the jobs he took were often strenuous, and the pay was low, Bruno stayed focused on his intent to complete his college education. Twice during the seven years he needed to earn his degree, Bruno was forced to take a leave of absence to replenish his savings. During his last semester, when he was close to graduating, Bruno petitioned the university to be allowed to finish his course requirements remotely while he started a job as a municipal secretary at the town of Tänassilma. While working full-time, he completed his academic coursework and was finally awarded a law degree from the University of Tartu in the spring of 1939.

At the time when Bruno was starting his new career, he decided to follow the example of the many Estonians who were changing their surnames to emphasize their Estonian heritage. Taking advantage of an opportunity offered by the Estonian government, Bruno chose to "estonianize" his last name by adding Kulgma to his surname of Kull.

My mother shared few details regarding how and when Bruno's widowed mother died other than to say she had been ill for a while. Rather than move, Bruno decided after his mother's death to continue leasing the apartment they shared on the second floor of the Vares family home. He was now alone in the world, yet confident in his abilities and determined to pursue a career devoted to Estonian law.

There are only a few pictures of Bruno in the family albums and none that show Bruno and Asta together as a couple. As I went through the photographs, I noticed one group shot where Asta had evidently cut out the space where Bruno's face would have appeared. My mother and I discovered the cropped picture in a gold locket that Asta wore as a high school student. Even before they became romantically involved, Asta evidently harbored a secret crush on the hard-working renter who lived on the second floor of her family home.

Bruno was tall, handsome, intelligent, and more mature than many of the other young men Asta knew. She must surely have noticed that even though he was ambitious and hard-working, he rarely thought about himself and was considerate of others. My mother remembered that besides being very smart, Bruno had a great sense of humor and was fun to be around.

Based on how my mother described her sister, Asta and Bruno appeared to be kindred spirits. Both were principled, self-effacing, and immensely patriotic. Both were also committed to having careers that entailed helping others. Although neither Asta nor Bruno was looking for a serious romantic relationship, they would have realized as they spent time together that their goals for the future were very much intertwined.

In 1937 during the Christmas holidays, Asta took a family picture to commemorate my mother's sixteenth birthday. When Mom and I looked at the photo years later, she laughed when I asked why she was wearing earmuffs.

"I had an ear infection that would not go away. So, my father created a plaster cast to keep my ears warm and insisted that I wear a scarf around my neck."

In the photo, Bruno was twenty-three and facing his first Christmas alone after his mother's death. His shirt was rumpled, and his tie was slightly askew. With dark circles under his eyes, he stared at the camera with a half-smile. Enno and another unnamed family friend also posed for the group shot which Asta later saved in her album.

Bruno, Kaia, and Enno behind
a family friend, Christmas in Viljandi, 1937

Following tradition, Bruno would have joined other Estonians on that Christmas Eve to commemorate their deceased relatives by lighting candles on their graves. As he watched the hundreds of tiny flames flickering in the cold wintery night, Bruno must have felt very alone as he said farewell to his mother at her gravesite.

Over the next few months, my grandmother started to notice that Asta was attracted to Bruno, an infatuation she worried might derail her daughter's career. Moreover, from my grandmother's perspective, Bruno had no family connections, was working to put himself through college, and had a less than clearcut future. To head off the budding romance, my grandmother urged my mother to discourage the relationship, but Asta was undeterred. The future she wanted for herself was one that Bruno also shared, a future they planned to pursue together.

In June 1938, Asta graduated from high school with top-scoring grades. To celebrate her upcoming enrollment as a medical student at the University of Tartu, Asta arranged for a group photo to be taken in the backyard of the Vares family home. For the occasion, she wore a breezy summer dress and stood in a coy, flirtatious pose. Leaning into the group, Bruno linked arms with my mother while wearing a carefree expression, in contrast with his more somber pose during the Christmas holidays.

Bruno, Kaia, Enno, Asta, and two guests, Viljandi, 1938

In September Bruno and Asta both moved to Tartu to attend the university. Even though they were most likely engrossed in their studies, they would surely have noticed the ominous signs that war was brewing in Germany. After annexing Austria in March of 1938, Hitler occupied the Sudetenland in Czechoslovakia. Only six months later, he moved to take full control over the remaining provinces of Czechoslovakia in March of 1939.

Many students who were attending the University of Tartu during the 1938-39 academic year were alarmed when the Western countries failed to react after Hitler absorbed Austria and Czechoslovakia into the Third Reich. Even though the leaders of France and Great Britain were concerned over Hitler's ambitions, they wanted to believe that the German chancellor would be appeased by his territorial gains, but Hitler soon showed the world that he had even greater aspirations.

In the summer of 1939, Hitler ordered his foreign minister, Joachim von Ribbentrop, to negotiate a mutual assistance agreement with the Soviet foreign minister, Vyacheslav Molotov. The public-facing details of the resulting Molotov-Ribbentrop Pact merely stipulated that neither Germany nor the Soviet Union would come to the aid of any country that was an enemy to the other. Yet, the agreement also contained a secret protocol that erased the independence of Estonia, Latvia, and Lithuania with the stroke of a pen.

Without knowing the details of the agreement that Hitler and Stalin reached, the citizens of the Baltic countries were anxious about their future. Their fears were well-founded. On September 1, 1939, the German army marched into Poland. Two weeks later, the Red Army advanced into Polish territory from the east, stopping at a previously agreed-upon border that divided Poland between Germany and the U.S.S.R.

The sobering reality that Poland, like Austria and Czechoslovakia, could so easily lose its independence set a worrisome precedent for Estonia, which had only become a sovereign country in 1918. Over the two decades prior to the war, the Soviet Union had conspired on several occasions to undermine Estonia's independence. After Poland's democratic government had been so quickly overthrown, many Estonians questioned what the fate of their own small country might be. The Soviets would soon provide an answer.

In late September, Vyacheslav Molotov demanded that Estonian Foreign Minister Karl Selter, travel to Moscow for an urgent meeting. According to Selter's written record, Molotov started the session by complaining that political relations between the Soviet Union and Estonia had substantially deteriorated.

"Estonia gained sovereignty when the Soviet Union was powerless," Molotov asserted. "But you don't think that this can last forever…. The Soviet Union is now a great power whose interests need to be taken into consideration. I tell you—the Soviet Union needs enlargement of her security guarantee system; for this purpose, she needs an exit to the Baltic Sea…. I ask you, do not compel us to use force against Estonia."[10]

In response to Molotov's outburst, Selter pointed out that Estonia was a neutral country. Any agreement that the small Baltic nation might make with the Soviet Union would violate the non-aggression treaty Estonia had previously established with Germany.

Molotov retorted that since the Soviet Union also had a non-aggression pact with Germany, he was confident that the German officials would not complain if the U.S.S.R. and Estonia developed an agreement to protect the security of Soviet shipping in the Baltic Sea. Rather than sign the agreement, Selter argued that the final terms would need to be approved by the president of Estonia and the country's parliament.

---

10   "Karl Selter," Wikipedia.

Molotov responded by insisting that the Estonians reach an agreement on his proposal with no delay.

"I stress once more: the matter is urgent. The situation needs an immediate solution. We cannot wait long. I advise you to accede to the wishes of the Soviet Union in order to avoid something worse."

Molotov then issued an ominous warning,

"Do not compel the Soviet Union to use force to achieve her aims."[11]

Later that evening, Molotov called the Estonian diplomatic team back to his office to share a draft of the written agreement the Soviet foreign minister expected them to ratify. Before they left, the Soviet foreign minister tried to assuage any worry the Estonian diplomats might have by asserting that the Soviet Union did not intend to infringe in the slightest degree on the sovereignty of Estonia or the country's independence.

Three days later, when Selter returned to Moscow, he asked Molotov to reconsider the terms of the agreement, since the treaty would result in a military occupation of Estonia. To mollify Selter's concerns, Molotov invited Joseph Stalin to join the meeting. Stalin echoed the demands that his foreign minister had made and insisted that the Estonians needed to sign the agreement.

"The placing of Red Army units into Estonia according to the proposal presented today is absolutely necessary. Otherwise," Stalin warned, "the Soviet naval and air bases

---

11 *Lithuanian Quarterly Journal*, "Minutes of the Soviet-Estonian Negotiations."

could not feel themselves secure during the present time of war."

To further reassure the hesitant Estonian diplomats, Stalin promised,

"This is only a wartime measure. At the end of the war, we will bring back these troops."

As the Estonian legation listened to the Soviet demands, they realized that the leaders of the Soviet Union intended to achieve their objectives, irrespective of whether Estonia ratified the defense agreement or not. After further negotiations, the Soviets agreed to reduce the size of the Soviet military garrisons and to restrict their troop movements to the agreed-upon military installations. Despite these concessions, the Estonian diplomats knew they had no leverage with which to resist the Soviet demands and with deep reservation, they finally agreed to sign the treaty.

Stalin congratulated the Estonians for ratifying the mutual assistance pact between the two countries and reminded them what might have happened to their country if they had not agreed to the Soviet terms.

"I can tell you that the Estonian government did wisely and well in the interests of the Estonian people by concluding the agreement with the Soviet Union." Stalin then added, "It could have happened to you what happened to Poland. Poland was a great country. Where is Poland now?... I tell you frankly that you acted well and in the interests of your people."[12]

---

12 *Lithuanian Quarterly Journal.* "Minutes of the Soviet-Estonian Negotiations."

Within a matter of weeks, diplomats from Latvia and Lithuania were forced to sign similar mutual assistance pacts with the U.S.S.R. Shortly after the treaty with Estonia was finalized, the Soviets moved twenty-five thousand Red Army troops across Estonia's borders in October of 1939. They also started constructing military bases on two Estonian islands and at the port of Paldiski.[13]

My mother said Estonians were outraged when Soviet troops crossed over Estonia's borders, but they also recognized that the Estonian army could not fight against the vastly superior Soviet forces. None of the Baltic states had the military strength to resist the Soviet demands. Nor could they count on any help from other Western nations.

After the Red Army troops began constructing military bases on Estonian soil, many Estonians tried to find ways to resist the Soviet aggression. At the University of Tartu, Bruno joined the Estonian Students' Society (ESS), a fraternity known for its nationalist fervor. Throughout its history, the ESS brothers had been strong defenders of Estonia's status as a sovereign country, and they resolved once again to fight against the Soviet incursion. Bruno enthusiastically joined their efforts.

The Christmas season of 1939 was an anxious time when Estonia, like Austria, Czechoslovakia, and Poland, was on the brink of being assimilated within a larger, more powerful neighbor. Finnish leaders, seeing the threat posed by the Soviet defense treaties, refused to agree to the Soviet demands, leading the U.S.S.R. to declare war against Finland.

---

13   Bultar, *Between Giants: The Battle for the Baltics'*

After the Soviets invaded Finland at the end of November, the Finns put up a valiant resistance and repelled the Soviet attacks throughout the winter. Inspired by the heroic resistance shown by the Finnish defenders, many Estonian men crossed the Baltic Sea to join them in their fight against the Soviet army.

Despite the worrisome news that pervaded their holiday celebrations, Bruno and Asta became engaged. They were deeply in love and excited about building a future life together even though they did not know when it might be feasible for them to marry. No one could anticipate when Estonia's independence would be restored. Yet, whatever the future might bring, Asta and Bruno resolved to face their challenges together.

CHAPTER 7

THE SOVIETS TAKE OVER

At the start of 1940, Bruno was gratified when he finally earned his law degree and could begin saving money. For her part, Asta was excited to be completing the course requirements for her second year of medical school. When she had the opportunity to return to Viljandi, she set out to help her father in his office and to experience what it would be like when she, too, could begin seeing her own patients.

The presence of the Soviet soldiers was aggravating, but many Estonians chose to believe the Soviets were only interested in establishing a military presence in Estonia and nothing more. Yet, the news reports covering the Soviet occupation in Poland were ominous.

Shortly after occupying eastern Poland in the fall of 1939, the Soviets staged forced elections to legitimize their annexation. To assure the takeover proceeded smoothly, the Soviet Secret Police detained anyone considered to be a threat to Soviet rule. Poland's top military officers, political leaders, government officials, and intellectuals were executed while soldiers in the Polish military were sent to the Soviet Gulag.

In addition to eliminating Poland's top leaders, the Soviets moved to deport large numbers of Polish citizens. In February, Soviet troops supervised the transport of 220,000 Polish men, women, and children to slave labor camps in Siberia. Only a few months later, 320,000 Poles were deported to Kazakhstan. To consolidate their control over the Polish economy, the Soviets began the process of collectivizing Polish farms. They also outlawed organizations that were associated with Polish culture or the former Polish state.[14]

Through their aggressive actions, the Soviets made it clear that they intended to destroy Poland and, in the process, eliminate large segments of Polish society. Estonians watched nervously, wondering if this was the same fate the Soviets intended for their country as well. By the summer, the Soviet plans for the three Baltic countries became clear.

While the Western world was riveted by the sight of Wehrmacht soldiers marching through the streets of Paris, one hundred thousand Soviet troops encircled Estonia, Latvia, and Lithuania by land and by sea on June 17, 1940. After blocking access to Baltic harbors, Soviet tanks, armored vehicles, and military transport trucks swarmed through local towns and villages.[15]

My mother remembered being shocked when she saw Russian soldiers taking up command posts in front of the Viljandi town hall. They were dirty, grungy, and unwelcome,

---

14   "Soviet Repressions of Polish Citizens (1939-1946)," Wikipedia.

15   Estonian International Commission. "Phase 1: The Soviet Occupation of Estonia."

and Mom said she did her best to ignore them whenever she walked through town.

Like many Estonians, Mom hoped she could continue her day-to-day life. But within a short time, it was obvious that the Soviets intended to annex Estonia as a Socialist state. Although Estonia's President Konstantin Päts was initially allowed to stay in power, the Soviets demanded that he sign nearly two hundred decrees including one that announced a new national election that was scheduled to be held in July.

The Soviets also demanded that Päts appoint Moscow's preferred candidate, Johannes Vares Barbarus, as the country's prime minister. A month later, when Päts was forced to resign, Vares Barbarus took his place as the president of Estonia's Soviet controlled government.

According to my mother, Johannes Vares Barbarus was my grandfather's cousin. Born a year after my grandfather, Johannes grew up twelve miles from my grandfather's family farm. The two cousins both travelled to Russia to study medicine. While Johannes studied at the University of Kyiv, my grandfather received his training at the University of Moscow. After becoming doctors, both cousins served as physicians in Russia's Imperial Army during World War I. Upon his return to Estonia, Johannes set up a medical practice as a gynecologist in the town of Pärnu and my grandfather became an internist in Viljandi.

While their early life experiences were similar, the two cousins had opposing political views. After studying in the Soviet Union, Johannes admired the Soviet system and wrote essays criticizing what he called Estonia's bourgeois nationalism. By contrast, my grandfather was a staunch Estonian patriot who became part of the cadre of leaders who guided Estonia's growth as an independent democracy after the War of Independence ended.

Once Vares Barbarus was installed as Estonia's president, the Pärnu physician may have believed that the Soviets would permit Estonia to retain some independence, but he soon realized the Soviets intended to blot out any evidence that Estonia had ever been a sovereign nation.

As they had done in Poland, the Soviets arranged national elections to legitimize their control over the Estonian government. As the July elections were being organized, only trustworthy Communist candidates who were pre-approved by Moscow were allowed to be included on the ballots. When eighty-seven Estonian nationalists attempted to compete for the open parliamentary positions, the Soviet officials disqualified them based on technicalities or arrested them for committing anti-Soviet offenses. The only Estonian candidate, Jüri Rajur-Liivak, who was successful in having his name placed on the national ballot, was arrested after the election on a false charge of forgery and remained in prison for two weeks.

My grandparents were staunch Estonian nationalists, who abhorred the Soviet demands that they vote for the Communist slate of candidates, but they had no choice. Prior to the election, the Soviets announced that voting was a civic responsibility. Those who refused risked being put on trial as traitors to the people.

Confident of the election outcome, Soviet emissaries shared the names of the winning candidates with a London-based newspaper several hours before the results were declared in Estonia.[16] A year later, German investigators confirmed that pro-Soviet poll watchers forged more than thirty-five thousand ballots, counted invalid votes, and switched the tallies for Liivak to other Communist Party candidates.[17]

To the many Estonians who had fought for their country's independence, the forced election was a painful validation that the Soviets were in full control. As a small country with a prewar population of one million residents,[18] Estonia had a tight-knit society in which the country's leaders, despite their political differences, were friends, political colleagues, and compatriots. Through his civic involvement, my grandfather had working relationships with many of Estonia's top politicians.

After the staged election, when the Moscow-approved Estonian assembly petitioned the U.S.S.R. to recognize Estonia as a Soviet Socialist Republic, my grandfather along with Estonia's other leaders, would have been heartbroken. Yet, beyond the loss of their country, they soon realized their own lives were threatened.

Within months of occupying Estonia, the Soviet Secret Police arrested eight thousand government officials, lawmakers, military leaders, and police officers and accused them of trying to overthrow, undermine, and weaken the power of the U.S.S.R. The Soviet Secret Police later executed one in four of those who were arrested.[19]

---

16 Estonian State Commission. "The White Book."

17 "1940 Estonian Parliamentary Election," Wikipedia.

18 "List of Countries by Population in 1939," Wikipedia.

19 Laar, *Red Terror.*

The Estonian leaders were brought before Soviet-controlled tribunals and tried under a Soviet-imposed legal system that defined Estonian nationalism as a crime against the U.S.S.R. The Soviet code of justice also imposed death sentences on those defendants who were found guilty of being loyal to the Estonian state.

Because of his role in Viljandi's local government, my grandfather must have worried that he, too, could be among those who were detained, particularly after his brother, Jakob, was taken into custody. Prior to the Soviet occupation, Jakob had served as the Viljandi Chief of Police for nearly a decade. Even though he resigned from his post when the Communists took over, he was arrested in mid-September. A short time later, a second brother, Elmar, disappeared after he was transported to a Soviet prison.

Beyond the terror associated with the widescale arrests, Estonians were apprehensive over the Soviet plans to reorganize the country's economy. After Estonia was incorporated into the U.S.S.R., the newly installed government moved to nationalize the country's banks, to take over industrial plants, and to collectivize privately-owned farms. The pronouncements made it clear that the Communist Party intended to control how the country functioned and which Estonians could keep their jobs. Local Estonian leaders found themselves powerless to resist the policies that the Soviets were imposing.

When the head of the Communist Party in Viljandi asked Bruno if he was interested in becoming a Party member, Bruno realized this could be his opportunity to help the Estonian cause. Mom said that the Party leaders considered Bruno to be an attractive candidate as they set out to take charge of Viljandi's government.

"Since very few Estonians belonged to the Communist Party," Mom said, "The Party leaders were eager to find new recruits, and they liked Bruno because he was young, smart, and had a college degree. Bruno was exactly the type of person they believed could give the Party some legitimacy."

Eager to find ways to undermine the Communist Party's ambitions, Bruno approached several of Viljandi's civic leaders for their advice. Those he contacted included the Governor of Viljandi County, several members of the Viljandi City Council, a local judge, as well as my grandfather. All of them supported Bruno's decision to accept the risky assignment while also warning him to be careful.

Being young and self-assured, Bruno believed he could gain the confidence of the Communist Party leaders while hiding his true allegiances. Many were old-guard Party members who had little experience in local government, and they welcomed Bruno's help. While pretending to be enthusiastic about the Party's plans, Bruno set out to subvert their take-over efforts while keeping Viljandi's leaders informed.

In Tartu, Bruno's fellow fraternity brothers at the Estonian Students' Society were making similar plans to infiltrate, sabotage, and thwart the Soviet occupiers. One ESS member who was fluent in Russian volunteered to become a chauffeur for the local Party officials to overhear their conversations. The fraternity brothers also set up an observation post to identify the would-be collaborators who visited the building where the Soviet Secret Police, also known as the NKVD, had established their headquarters.

From the start of the Soviet occupation, the Soviet Secret Police instituted aggressive methods for identifying those who resisted the newly installed Soviet regime. After Andres

Raska, an ESS fraternity brother, was arrested for distributing blue, black, and white ribbons to thirty people at a Tartu protest meeting, an NKVD tribunal sentenced him to a six-year prison term. He died in the Kirov prison a few months after his arrival. [20]

In Viljandi, my mother remembered how shaken my grandfather was when he returned one day from the local jail where he was summoned by the Soviet Secret Police to care for an inmate. When my grandfather returned home, Mom said his face was ashen as he shook his head and said there was nothing he could do. The NKVD agents had cut out the tongue of the banker's son when he could not reveal where his father had hidden the bank's gold reserves.

Even the simplest forms of protest were severely punished. When 24-year-old Karl Sinijärv distributed thirty leaflets and hoisted the Estonian flag at a Tallinn demonstration, a Soviet tribunal gave him a ten-year prison sentence. For the crime of trying to remove election posters in Rakvere, Aadu Allvee and his brother Simo were transported to a Russian labor camp where Aadu died a year later. Three other students lost their lives in Russian prisons because they sang anti-Soviet songs and removed wreaths from Communist graves in Tallinn.[21]

Beyond punishing all forms of dissent, the new Soviet authorities made it clear that loyalty to the Communist Party was a prerequisite for Estonians who wanted to stay employed. Those who occupied top leadership positions were expected

---

20   Niitsoo, "The Nonviolent Resistance to the Soviet Occupation."

21   Niitsoo, "The Nonviolent Resistance to the Soviet Occupation."

to show their allegiance to the Soviet regime by becoming members of the Communist Party.

Within the local school system, teachers were obligated to teach classes on Soviet history and the Russian language. Those suspected of being nationalist sympathizers were fired. Students who protested were treated even more harshly.

When Johan Koop and Erick Talve, students at the Valga Industrial School, distributed leaflets that read "Down with Communism," the Soviet-controlled courts sentenced them to five years in prison. They were luckier than the four students from Viljandi High School who were executed at Kirov prison for distributing leaflets calling for Estonians to overthrow the Soviet occupation. [22]

Given the severity with which the Soviets punished any form of disloyalty, Asta must have worried about what might happen if the Party leaders discovered that Bruno was acting as a spy for Viljandi's town leaders. Being a fastidious lawyer, Bruno explained that he had made sure that there were few people in Viljandi who knew what his true loyalties were when he joined the Communist Party.

Like his fellow fraternity brothers, Bruno believed that once Hitler invaded the Soviet Union, he would finally be able to reveal his true allegiances and to explain to his neighbors and others in the town of Viljandi how he had been working to defend his fellow Estonians.

Even though he was careful to keep up his masquerade, Bruno would likely have found it difficult to conceal his Estonian sympathies. Mom remembered how angry Bruno

---

22   Niitsoo, "The Nonviolent Resistance to the Soviet Occupation."

was one night when he joined the Vares family for dinner. Earlier in the day, he told them, he heard that the Soviets intended to destroy the granite memorial in Viljandi's town square that honored the veterans who fought in the Estonian War of Independence. While Bruno complained about how the Soviets were trying to eliminate Estonia's past, my mother became indignant.

Being nineteen years old and impulsive, Mom decided to recruit a friend to help her protect the memorial. After sneaking out later that night, the two girls stood at the statue's foundation, falsely believing that the Red Army soldiers would not dare to blow it up if two teenagers were standing nearby. When there was no sign of the Soviet troops, Mom and her friend returned home several hours later.

The girls were discouraged, particularly when the statue was blown up the following afternoon. Yet, they were lucky not to have been detained by the Soviet Secret Police. In another part of the country four teenagers, Boris Treimann, Villem Kivi, Otto Sepp, and Sigurd Papisoo, received multi-year prison sentences when they tried to protect an Estonian memorial.

Another protestor, Karl Palm, was even less fortunate. After Palm tried to stop the Soviets from destroying a monument, the 18-year-old was brutally killed while in custody. When his lifeless corpse was returned, his parents found that their son's face had been bloodied beyond recognition and all the bones in his fingers were broken.

Even though Bruno was aware that he risked being uncovered by the Soviet Secret Police, he decided to take a leadership position within the Communist Party by becoming the head of the Nominating Committee. From this post,

Bruno knew that he could recommend which candidates the Party would approve for various jobs within the courts, local businesses, and the schools. Being the head of the Nominating Committee also ensured that Bruno could fill certain leadership positions with colleagues that he trusted from the university.

After setting up an application system, Bruno came to know what credentials would guarantee that those applying for jobs would be approved by the Communist Party leaders. He coached Estonian job seekers on how to apply for jobs and then spoke up for them when their loyalties were questioned.

Recognizing the risk Bruno faced if his ruse was discovered, Asta urged her fiancé to keep a low profile, but Bruno remained confident that the Communist Party leaders trusted him. Knowing that they relied on his skills, he decided to redouble his efforts by volunteering to serve as the Party Secretary.

From this position, Bruno could intercept any complaint letters that charged prominent town leaders with having anti-Communist views. One of the letters he later destroyed accused my grandfather of being a bourgeois nationalist because he permitted patients in his waiting room to criticize the Soviet army.

Cognizant of the ever-present surveillance network that the Soviet Secret Police created, Bruno was discrete when he sent warnings to those Estonians who were under surveillance. He was also careful to cover his tracks when he passed along information to Viljandi's civic leaders and took extra precautions to protect his fellow ESS fraternity brothers whenever they met.

Over time, as he became more familiar with the inner workings of Viljandi's Communist Party, Bruno decided to take even more drastic steps to disrupt their operations. On several occasions, he circulated rumors that were designed to incite petty rivalries between the Party officials and their counterparts in the Soviet Secret Police and the Red Army. He also publicized the complaints he received that denounced top Communist officials, particularly when their loyalty was called into question.

Even though Bruno believed his position within the Communist Party provided him with some protection, he was aware that he would be sentenced to death if his surreptitious activities were discovered. The sobering reality of how easily his true allegiances could be revealed became evident to both Bruno and Asta when the Soviet Secret Police uncovered an underground protest movement founded by Ülo Maramaa, the son of Viljandi's long-time Mayor, August Maramaa.

Like Bruno, Ülo became determined to resist the Soviet occupation shortly after the national elections were held. When his efforts to place Estonian nationals on the July ballot failed, the 30-year-old activist conspired with other Estonian loyalists to form a nationwide resistance network called the Salvation Committee. Together, they developed a twenty-point plan that specified how Estonians could regain control over the country's institutions once the German army forced the Soviets to retreat. The Committee members also sought to acquire weapons by reaching out to Estonian soldiers who were fighting in Finland.

Despite the precautions the Committee members took to limit those who knew about their activities, the Soviet Secret Police arrested Ülo Maramaa and some of his fellow conspirators on December 30, 1940. Even though Ülo possessed two poison pills, he was unable to use them before the police arrived. He decided to cooperate when the NKVD threatened to harm his family and fellow conspirators.

During his initial interrogations, Ülo tried to minimize the activities of the Salvation Committee by testifying that they met only to exchange information. While he admitted that he attempted to contact German diplomats in Tallinn, Ülo pointed out that his efforts were unsuccessful. He also testified that his transmitter was too weak to contact the Estonian soldiers who were fighting in Finland.

Under pressure from the NKVD investigators, Ülo eventually named the nine leaders who headed the local chapters of the Salvation Committee. He also identified the organizer who managed the network's youth branch. Based on Ülo's testimony, the Soviet Secret Police arrested 119 Estonians who were involved with the Committee's activities and charged them with conspiracy against the Soviet regime.[23] After a Soviet tribunal found Ülo and fourteen of his fellow dissenters guilty, they were sentenced to death.

Other members of Ülo's family were also detained. Shortly after Ülo was imprisoned, his pregnant wife, Gerda Murre, was arrested at the theater where she was about to perform in a Johann Strauss operetta. After she was taken into custody, Gerda later wrote that she was interrogated in Russian, a language she did not speak. While she was being questioned, the Soviet guards punched and kicked her. Although her face

---

23   Niitsoo, "Unarmed Resistance."

was covered in blood and she lost several teeth, her biggest worry was that her unborn child might die.[24]

Shortly after Ülo was arrested, his father, August Maramaa, was also jailed, brought to trial, and given a nine-year prison sentence for engaging in anti-Soviet activities. Ulo's mother, Anna, was later arrested in June during the first wave of Soviet deportations.

Asta must have been shaken when she heard that Ulo and his father, August, had been arrested by the NKVD. During his tenure on the Viljandi City Council, my grandfather worked closely with August Maramaa. If Viljandi's former mayor and his family could be charged with treason against the Soviet Union for supporting the cause of Estonian independence, Asta realized that she and her father were both at risk for helping Bruno.

For his part, Bruno remained confident in his ability to fool the local Communist Party leaders. As evidence of their trust in him, he was given a substantial amount of independent discretion, particularly regarding the applicants he nominated to become members of the Communist Party.

Yet, at the start of the new year when a Russian official named Müürsepp arrived in Viljandi to take charge over the Communist Party, Bruno came under scrutiny. Some Party members began whispering that the brash young lawyer was untrustworthy while other avid Communists complained that despite their stellar credentials, their membership applications had been rejected. Bruno, his accusers alleged, showed favoritism by awarding the most lucrative jobs to his friends.

---

24   *Eesti Päevaleht*, "Primadonna was arrested."

Under the ever-watchful eye of Chairman Müürsepp, Bruno's masquerade was becoming perilous, particularly since other Estonians had been sentenced to death for far less serious crimes. Yet, Bruno also knew that he would come under suspicion if he tried to leave the Communist Party. After redoubling his efforts to hide any evidence that would cause the Soviet Secret Police to question his loyalties, he could only hope that Viljandi's Party leaders would continue to trust him despite the detractors who questioned his motives.

CHAPTER 8

THE SOVIETS CLAMP DOWN

Bruno did not have to wait long before Müürsepp decided his fate. Rather than turning Bruno's case over to the NKVD, the Soviet leader determined that the young attorney could be more useful to the Party by taking over the very visible post of Party Chairman. To test Bruno's claim that he was indeed a staunch defender of Bolshevik ideology, Müürsepp invited him to demonstrate his loyalty to the Communist Party by giving speeches and writing newspaper articles.

In place of the anonymous role that Bruno had played in the past, his new position forced him to become a Communist sympathizer on a very public stage. While Bruno would appear to be the spokesperson for the Communist Party, and its most visible leader, Müürsepp still retained full control over the Party's operations.

Bruno could not refuse. Leaving the Party was not an option. Nor could he decline the new position which Müürsepp described as a promotion. Any sign that Bruno was reluctant to become the Party's public spokesperson would only confirm that Bruno was someone who could not be trusted. Any hint of his true antipathy toward the Communist Party would lead to his arrest by the Soviet Secret Police who had placed Bruno under surveillance based on the complaints that were lodged against him.

Reluctantly, Bruno began giving public lectures where he tried to talk about Bolshevik theory in the blandest possible terms. In one newspaper article, he described the layout of a public reading room, noting that the material related to the Communist Party was available only in the Russian language.

Despite his carefully balanced efforts to avoid promoting Communism or the Soviet occupation, Bruno found that his Estonian neighbors were, nonetheless, labelling him as a Party loyalist who espoused Communist ideology. Few knew about the Estonians Bruno had helped or about the complaint letters he had destroyed.

Instead, most believed that Bruno was closely affiliated with the hated Soviet occupiers who were ruining their lives. His friends from high school looked at him in disbelief while his neighbors shunned him. For those who had suffered under the Soviet regime and lost loved ones, Bruno was an easy target for their anger and disgust, a very public scapegoat for those who reviled the Soviets and the harm they were causing.

As Bruno continued to write favorable newspaper articles about the Communist Party, Viljandi's civic leaders warned him to downplay his public appearances. Yet, under the ever-watchful eye of the NKVD, Bruno knew he needed to continue his charade. He had accepted a job that few of his associates were willing to assume. Those he tried to recruit to take his place all decided the position carried too much personal risk.

While Bruno struggled in his role as the Communist Party Chairman, Asta remained his steady confidant, the one person with whom he could share his frustration and his fears. She, more than anyone, recognized the sacrifice he was making. After he had worked for years to become a lawyer who defended Estonia's constitution, she knew that Bruno was being forced to promote a Communist ideology that was antithetical to his true beliefs.

When Asta noticed the dark-clothed NKVD agents who sometimes stood in the park next to the family's house, she became alarmed. She knew that Bruno was taking steps to eliminate any evidence that could be used against him, but she also recognized that many Estonians were being arrested based on evidence that was flimsy and unsubstantiated.

Despite Asta's fears, she was proud that Bruno was willing to sacrifice his life to defend Estonia's independence. His courage inspired her to also become involved in the informal resistance groups that were fighting against the Soviet occupation.

In one diary entry, she wrote, "Call and I'll rise from the grave should you need me, my fatherland."

Despite the risk that she could be implicated along with Bruno, Asta passed along the information Bruno gathered to warn those Estonians who were under surveillance. With the help of other patriotic resistors, she also established a network of safe houses on the outskirts of town where Estonians could hide from the Soviet Secret Police. To keep track of the locations, she sketched a cryptic outline in her diary, noting the initials of those refugees who were being sheltered at the various sites.

To avoid any possibility of being uncovered by the Soviet Secret Police, Bruno began destroying his files while alerting his fraternity brothers that he was being watched. Based on his experience within the Communist Party, he knew how easily the NKVD could discover his secret alliances. He also worried that the Soviets could also charge Asta with treason.

The dangers they faced became ever more apparent after an ESS fraternity brother was arrested and transported to a prison in Siberia. As the members of the resistance network watched and worried, no one knew who among them might be the next suspect to be detained. Despite the risks, the ESS fraternity brothers began meeting more frequently to discuss how they could sabotage Soviet military outposts, disrupt communication systems, and slow down the Red Army by damaging local railroads, when, as expected, the German invasion of the U.S.S.R. finally began.

While both Bruno and Asta were anxious about being discovered, the Vares family faced a separate threat from the Soviet Secret Police. After my grandfather's brother, Jakob, was arrested at the family farm, both of my grandparents frequently visited the Viljandi jail to bring him food and to check on his safety. Over months of incarceration, Jakob began having problems with kidney stones that caused him a great deal of discomfort.

To ease his brother's condition, my grandfather arranged to bring Jakob some pain medication, but the Soviet guards discovered the pills shortly after my grandparents arrived at the jail for one of their regular visits. Upon discovering the hidden medicine, the guards took my grandparents to separate rooms for questioning.

My grandfather told the guards that he was a doctor, who was just trying to help his brother, but my grandmother lied. When she was confronted with the evidence, she claimed that she did not know anything about the pills. Given the fact that the guards had already confiscated the pain medication, they told my grandmother that she would have to come back for more questioning by NKVD investigators.

When Mom told me the story about Jakob's pills, she explained that everyone in Viljandi knew stories about what happened to those who were interrogated by the NKVD. Independent of whether there was any questionable activity, some defendants were arrested without having access to a trial while others were forced to become informers.

Panicked over the prospect of being interrogated, my grandmother began pacing through the family apartment late into the night. Always one to overthink her problems, she must have spent hours rehearsing how she planned to respond when she was questioned about her evident lie regarding Jakob's pills. Perhaps she could claim she had made an innocent mistake. Perhaps she could point out that she had not committed any type of crime. Perhaps she could question how the NKVD could prove that she knew about the pills.

Whatever she might say and whatever excuse she might offer, she knew in the end, the NKVD investigators were unlikely to be convinced since they had most likely already decided that she was untrustworthy.

Even though Estonia's borders were heavily patrolled, my grandmother decided her family needed to escape. She proposed that they travel to one of Estonia's coastal towns where they could hire a boat to cross the Baltic Sea to Sweden. Other Estonians were making the trip and my grandfather, she reasoned, had connections. If they were careful, she was sure they could find a way to leave town without anyone noticing they had left.

When my grandmother announced her plan, Mom said, "There was a big fight. My father thought it was not safe to cross the Baltic and Asta just flat out refused to go. Since Bruno was unable to quit the Communist Party without drawing attention to himself, Asta insisted that she would not leave without him."

Undeterred, my grandmother began packing suitcases for the entire family even though she had no idea how they were going to escape. Little did she know that instead of scheduling her interrogation, the Soviet Secret Police were preoccupied with their efforts to secure the hundreds of cattle cars they needed to deport tens of thousands of Estonians in the upcoming week.

Few Estonians were aware that the Soviets planned to transport a broad cross-section of Estonian society, including men, women, and children to Siberia. According to Bruno's written testimony, the details regarding how and when the deportation was going to be conducted were kept secret, even from the Communist Party leaders.

After receiving quotas for each region that enumerated how many people needed to be arrested, the NKVD identified anyone suspected of being an Estonian patriot or to otherwise be a risk to the Soviet occupation. As the lists were being compiled, the process was so secretive that the Soviet Secret Police mistakenly included some Party loyalists on the deportation rolls.

There would be no trials and no opportunity for an appeal. In the end, being Estonian was enough to warrant an arrest, followed by deportation to destinations thousands of miles away. To consolidate their control over all the Baltic countries, the Soviets also planned to round up tens of thousands of civilians in Latvia and Lithuania.

Late in the evening of Friday, June 13, 1941, Russian guards accompanied by Red Army soldiers set out with their pre-prepared lists to detain the ten thousand Estonians who were targeted for deportation.[25] The deportees included former government officials, judges, bankers, business leaders, as well as police officers, and those who were associated with the Estonian military. In Viljandi, 750 men and women, including elderly retirees and children were forced to pack their suitcases without being told where they were going to be taken.[26] Fewer than half of those transported to Siberia ever returned home.[27]

The scale of the arrests across the Baltic states was staggering. In Latvia, 15,500 civilians were arrested, while another 17,500 were apprehended in Lithuania. All the deportees were sent to a network of distant Siberian towns and labor camps. The terror the deportees experienced must have been overwhelming. In one account, a survivor remembered how confused his parents were when Red Army soldiers banged on their doors well after the family had gone to bed.

"They ordered us to pack as many things as we could and said that we had to go and live somewhere else."

When his father asked what he had done to hurt anyone, he was told, "You are a class enemy, and we are going to annihilate you."[28]

---

25   *ERR.EE News,* "June 1941."

26   Memory and Conscience Conference 2016, "Viljandi."

27   Altau, "Baltic deportations."

28   Moorhouse, *The Devil's Alliance.*

While some of the arresting officers advised the deportees to bring along warm clothing and a supply of food, others were less helpful. The guards provided little information about where the deportees were going to be taken.

They were also careful not to alert the families that parents would be separated at the railroad station since the men were going to be shipped to labor camps while their families were transported to more distant Siberian towns on the far reaches of Russia's eastern borders.

My mother must have known many of those who were caught in the NKVD round-up. They included the town's most prominent business leaders, teachers from her high school, and politicians who served in local government along with my grandfather.

Neighbors who fought in the War of Independence were arrested, as well as anyone associated with the Red Cross and other organizations deemed by the Soviets to have Western affiliations. More than 70 percent of those arrested were women, children, and the elderly. One in four was under the age of sixteen.[29]

Throughout the town, neighbors and friends disappeared in the night. Families with young children were packed into railroad cars next to older retirees who questioned why they were being forced to leave their homes. Storekeepers, teachers, and local pastors found themselves accused of crimes they were unaware they had committed.

At the railroad stations, women cried in desperation when their husbands and fathers were placed in separate cars, not

---

29 Estonian World, "Estonian Remembers the Soviet Deportations."

knowing how they could stay in touch or when they might be reunited. As the deportees were crowded into the cattle cars, no one had any idea where they would be taken or how long they would be gone. They could not have known that those who were fortunate enough to survive would need to wait nearly a decade before they could return to Estonia.

When Estonian diplomats appealed to the United States to condemn the deportations, U.S. Under Secretary of State Sumner Welles expressed regret over the Soviet actions. In a written statement, he said the United States had "the deepest sympathy for all countries and people, including the country and people of Estonia, which have fallen as victims of aggression." Even so, he concluded it would serve no useful purpose to undertake any action to stop the Soviets.[30]

By deporting tens of thousands of Baltic residents, Stalin intended to uproot as many Estonians, Latvians, and Lithuanians as possible. Few provisions were made for food or housing at the Siberian destinations where the deportees were sent. They were not expected to survive and indeed many died during the harsh Siberian winters that ensued a few months after they arrived.

On that fateful June weekend, when my grandmother watched her friends and neighbors being escorted to the town's railroad station, her worry over her own situation must have deepened. Even though the Vares family members were not on the initial deportation list, she knew that the Soviet police had labeled her as someone who was suspicious and

---

30 US Department of State, "United States Diplomatic Papers, 1941."

unreliable. When the Soviets conducted their next deportation, my grandmother was sure her family would be among those who were arrested.

CHAPTER 9

THE DEPORTATIONS

Decades after World War II ended, I tried to imagine what it would have been like to discover one weekend that many of my neighbors, colleagues, and friends had been suddenly arrested and transported thousands of miles away. The residents of Viljandi were surely angry, resentful, and embittered over the indiscriminate arrests and deportations of their fellow Estonians who had committed no crimes.

Along with the grief they felt at losing many who were a part of their lives, they must also have had a deep worry that they, too, could be detained. Yet, despite their outrage, Estonians knew they had few options to fight against the Soviet threat. Moreover, there were no courts of law where they could demand that the Soviet deportations be condemned.

Over the years, my mother rarely spoke about the impact the deportations had on her family. Although they were spared, Mom revealed that my grandmother had a close friend who was deported to Siberia during the first Soviet round-up. The story emerged during one of my many visits to my parents' retirement home when my mother asked me to look over the remaining pieces of jewelry that she wanted me to consider taking.

The necklaces, earrings, and rings were mementos from a different place and a different time, too fancy for my laid-back lifestyle, but I humored my mother by looking through her collection.

After I picked up an ornate, gold ring with two interwoven strands that sparkled with small sapphires and diamonds, Mom explained that the ring had once belonged to my grandmother.

"This ring used to be two separate bands. Before the war, your grandmother and her best friend decided to purchase matching rings that they could wear together. Years later Grandmom had a jeweler intertwine the two strands."

"What happened to her friend?" I asked.

"She was deported," was all my mother said.

Mom had mentioned my grandmother's best friend, Irene Luik, on several other occasions. I knew that Irene and her husband, Johan, lived several houses down the street from my grandparents. Johan was a pharmacist who worked closely with my grandfather while Irene was my grandmother's dearest confidant.

Pictures from our family album show that the two families often socialized together. On one occasion, they snapped a smiling picture while vacationing at the beach town of Pärnu. Another time, Irene and my grandmother laughed while they posed in harem outfits to celebrate the New Year. The two families appeared enmeshed in the fabric of each other's lives. When my Uncle Jaan was born in 1929, Irene was the logical choice to become his godmother.

I learned more about the tragic fate of the Luik family when I travelled to Estonia in 2018. To commemorate the residents of the town who died during the two Soviet occupations, the Viljandi town museum worked with two other heritage organizations to compile stories that memorialized the lives of those residents of the town who had lost their lives.

The results were assembled in a dozen books entitled *"Sakalamaa Ei Unusta, Viljandi Linn"* (*The Homeland Does Not Forget, the Town of Viljandi*).[31] Within the eleventh volume in the series, I discovered a historical overview that captured the economic, political, and cultural life in Viljandi before the Soviets arrived. The thick paperback book also included a chronological listing of the names, dates, and ultimate fates of the town's residents who were victims of the Soviet repression.

In the section of the directory that enumerated the town's health care providers, my grandfather, Jaan Vares, was recorded as living in house number six on Lembitu Boulevard while the pharmacist, Johan Luik, resided in number 10 on the same street. Later sections of the book offered a brief history of the Luik family, as well as details regarding their deportation to Siberia.

Like many men in my grandfather's generation, Johan was described as having served with a front-line Estonian army unit during the country's War of Independence. In recognition of his service, the Estonian government gave him permission in 1922 to operate a pharmacy in Viljandi.

---

31   Piir, *Sakalamaa Ei Unusta, Viljandi Linn.*

During the years when Johan was establishing his drug store, my grandfather was building his medical practice in a nearby office space. Similar to the role my grandmother played supporting my grandfather in his office, Johan's wife, Irene, worked by her husband's side in the pharmacy. For the next twenty years, Johan and my grandfather collaborated with each other as prominent members of Viljandi's health care community.

On the warm June weekend when NKVD agents arrested nearly one thousand Viljandi residents, Johan and Irene Luik received their deportation orders on Saturday, June 14. After ordering them to report to the train station, the Soviet guards allowed them time to pack without telling the family where they were going or how long they would be gone.

Fearing the worst, Irene would have called my grandmother to let her know the fateful news that the Luik family had been told to report to the train station. Worried and frightened, Irene most likely struggled to decide what she should pack in the small suitcase that she was able to carry. How could she possibly anticipate what clothes she might need and how much food she should try to bring along?

Knowing my grandmother, I imagine she offered to help Irene by assuring her friend that she would send whatever clothes or food Irene might need once she arrived at her destination. The two friends could not have known what the future might bring. Recognizing that they might never see each other again, Irene must have given my grandmother the gold band that symbolized the many happy times they spent together, a ring that my grandmother cherished for the rest of her life.

When the Luik family reached the Viljandi railroad station, they were surrounded by several hundred bewildered men, women, and children who were all struggling to understand why they had been arrested. To Irene's alarm, Johan was ordered to join other Estonian men at one side of the tracks while she and her 18-year-old daughter, Laine, were shuttled to a different set of railroad cars.

After spending an uncomfortable night trying to sleep in the crowded boxcar, Irene watched throughout the next day as a never-ending line of anxious Estonians were herded through the station to the awaiting train cars. The hours passed slowly in the cramped, dusty compartment that barely allowed any of the passengers enough room to stretch their legs. As the daylight dwindled, when Irene could no longer hear the barking sound of the Soviet guard dogs, she settled in for another night of sleep.

Early on Monday morning, the passengers were relieved when the train began to move even though they remained fearful about what their future might be. Within a few hours, the train came to a halt at the Russian border. Irene could not have known that the cars in which Johan and other Estonian men were travelling were then uncoupled and rerouted to a northern rail line while the rest of the train continued eastward.

Records show that at the age of 53, Johan was transported to the Sosva prison camp in the Sverdlovsk Oblast where many Estonian diplomats, government officials, and military attaches were already in custody. After he disembarked, he did not know that his 46-year-old wife and teenage daughter were still on a train that would take them thousands of miles further away to the far eastern borders of Siberia.

When Irene and Laine reached the Tsinsky District in the Tomsk Oblast several days later, they were placed with other women in a rough bunkhouse and given instructions regarding where they were expected to work. Along with other deportees from Latvia and Lithuania, the women were assigned to a nearby lumber camp where they would be forced to labor from sunrise to sunset in exchange for their daily ration of food and water.

Anna Maramaa, Ülo's mother, was among the Viljandi residents transported to the Tomsk region. Under the harsh work requirements, she survived for only three years before dying on August 4, 1944, at the age of 60.

At the end of World War II, more than six years after members of the Luik family were taken to their respective labor camps, their daughter, Laine, managed to find her way back to Estonia in 1947. Laine lived in Estonia for two years before she was re-arrested by the Soviet Secret Police and sent back to Siberia in 1949. Before being transported for a second time, she arranged for some friends to care for her infant son. Over the course of the next four years, the family sent Laine regular updates regarding her son's progress, but she mourned the fact that her son was growing up without his mother by his side.

When she was interviewed in 1996, Laine remembered, "The family frequently sent pictures of my son. I no longer feel angry, but rather have a deep pain about this injustice. In Siberia, those who were deported survived because they believed they could return to their homeland. We were always waiting for something to change."[32]

Well after World War II ended, the Luik family continued to be incarcerated at their respective labor camps. In 1951, ten years after his initial arrest, Johan was transferred from Sosva to the Potma prison camp, located three hundred miles south of Moscow while his wife and daughter remained confined in Tomsk, two thousand miles away.

When Stalin died in 1954, Laine again received permission to return to Estonia, but her mother, Irene, was forced to remain in Tomsk where she died at the age of 59, nine months after Laine's release.

Once Laine returned to Estonia, she was eager to be reconnected with her father and tried to gain permission for his release and return to Estonia. Even though she submitted the requisite paperwork, the Soviet authorities would not allow Johan to return to his homeland.

During an interview, Laine recalled, "[My father] was scheduled to be released in October of 1955. While I waited for his return, I sent a statement to the camp officials explaining that I was prepared for him to arrive. Instead, he was sent to the Tomsk region even though he was disabled and incapacitated. By the time he reached the town of Kolpaseva, he was paralyzed and had to be hospitalized. He was later transferred to a home for the disabled where he died on April 13, 1961."[33]

---

32   Piir, *Sakalamaa Ei Unusta, Viljandi Linn.*

33   Piir, *Sakalamaa Ei Unusta, Viljandi Linn.*

After spending twenty years in captivity, Johan passed away at the age of 73, and was never able to reunite with his wife or daughter. Like many Estonians who were deported, he was buried in a distant Siberian cemetery far from his native land.

The stories of the Viljandi residents chronicled in *The Homeland Never Forgets* were haunting. Juxtaposed next to the smiling faces in wedding photos and family portraits were grim details regarding how each of the victims died. They were businessmen, teachers, judges, and poets until their lives were abruptly interrupted. While some Estonians were able to stay in touch with their families after they were deported, others merely disappeared. It was a fate that could have easily happened to my mother's family.

Asta did not comment on the June deportation in her diary. She, like many Estonians, would have been shocked by the impunity with which the Soviets arranged for tens of thousands of Estonians to be shipped to Siberia. She must also have worried that, when the Soviets organized their next deportation, her own family was likely to be among those who were arrested.

According to his written testimony, Bruno had no prior knowledge that the Soviets intended to arrest and deport nearly a thousand of Viljandi's residents. When the leaders of Communist Party complained about not being informed before the deportation occurred, the Soviet Secret Police responded by telling them that in the future, the deportation operations would be handled more efficiently.

According to Bruno, the NKVD bragged to the Communist Party leaders that the June deportation was just the beginning of a much larger effort. By the end of the summer, the Soviet Secret Police promised the Party leaders that all those Estonians they considered to be bourgeois nationalists would be eliminated. As devastating as the June deportation had been, the Soviets were planning an even more ambitious series of arrests.

From a legal perspective, Bruno knew that the Soviet deportations violated international law. The Soviets could offer no evidence that the ten thousand Estonians who were deported had committed any crimes. Nor were the deportees given an opportunity to defend themselves. Yet despite his outrage, Bruno could not openly challenge the Soviet authorities. Worse still, he remained the Party's spokesman.

To bolster his hope that, in some future time, he would have an opportunity to defend himself, Bruno started to identify witnesses who could speak on his behalf. He created a list that included the government workers, judges, doctors, hospital officials, and teachers who had been able to keep their jobs because of his intervention. He also named the farmers, business owners, and artists from Viljandi and Tänassilma who, without his help, would have otherwise come under suspicion by the Soviet authorities.

While he was preparing his written defense statement, Bruno chronicled the ways in which he subverted the Soviet occupation and described his many efforts to sabotage the Communist Party operations. Even though many in Viljandi viewed Bruno as a dedicated Communist, he hoped that the evidence he was gathering would prove his real motivations and the ways he had worked to defend Estonia's national interests.

Once the Soviets finally left, Bruno looked forward to explaining that he was forced to become the Party's spokesman after he came under suspicion by the Soviet Secret Police. He also anticipated that the Viljandi town leaders would vouch for his Estonian loyalties.

As he concluded his twenty-five-page defense testimony, Bruno wrote, "There are many who know me and my motives for joining the Party. They are also aware of my actions and my allegiances. Although the list of those I have helped includes some who were forcibly sent to Russia, I can also name other trusted people in Tallinn and Tartu if necessary. I have tried to explain my intent and to provide a listing of all those I have tried to help. The information should provide some understanding for my actions and what I hoped to achieve."

Despite Bruno's confidence that he could defend himself, Asta was disheartened. The June deportation had demonstrated how vulnerable her family was, particularly after Bruno told her that the Soviets were planning a second deportation. She tried to stay positive, but she also knew that Bruno's position was still tenuous. While the Communist Party leaders distrusted him, he was being scorned by many of his Estonian neighbors for his association with the hated the Soviet regime.

In her diary, Asta transcribed a poem by Marie Under that captured her despair.

> Days do not crumble to dust
> They flow not by like the water
> Some lay heavy on the heart
> Some will mark you forever.

As many Estonians tried to adjust to the traumatic loss of their relatives, neighbors, and friends at the hand of the

Soviets, they became heartened a week later when Hitler ordered three million German soldiers to attack the U.S.S.R. on June 22, 1941. The invasion force stretched across an eighteen-hundred-mile battlefront from the Baltic Sea to the borders of Ukraine.[34] While the Soviets were caught off guard by the German offensive, Estonians were euphoric.

My mother recalled, "Everybody was thrilled when we heard the German army had attacked the Soviet Union because we all believed that, once the Germans forced the Soviets to retreat, Estonia would be free again. We considered the Germans to be our saviors."

After hearing how quickly the Germans were advancing, my grandmother was elated and began unpacking the family suitcases. All her worries about being interrogated by the NKVD disappeared, since she assumed the Germans would soon force the Soviet occupiers to leave Estonia.

When he heard the news, Bruno was gratified that he could finally reveal his true allegiances as an Estonian patriot. For her part, Asta expected that shortly after the Soviets were gone, her fiancée and the other members of his resistance network would finally be recognized for their heroic efforts on behalf of the Estonian cause. Or so she wanted to believe.

---

34 U.S. Holocaust Memorial Museum, "Invasion of the Soviet Union, June 1941."

CHAPTER 10

THE SUMMER WAR

The Estonians I have known throughout my life have all been strongly patriotic and resolute in their commitment to preserving their Estonian identity. On the occasions when we gathered with other Estonians, I came to expect that a banquet array of Estonian food would be offered, followed by rousing Estonian songs.

My appreciation for the enduring love that Estonians have for their native land was deepened when I visited my Aunt Ester's Estonian relatives in Sweden. Prior to the outbreak of World War II, Ester's father, Jaak, and his wife, Leida, were fortunate to have settled in Stockholm, a mere three hundred miles across the Baltic Sea from Tallinn, Estonia's capital city.

Despite Sweden's proximity to Estonia, the couple discovered that soon after World War II began, they could no longer return to their homeland. After the Baltic Sea became one of the most heavily mined waters in the world, travel to Estonia was perilous. At the end of the war, when the Soviets began their postwar occupation of Estonia, the trip became impossible.

On the evening I arrived in Stockholm, Jaak and Leida celebrated my visit with a four-course meal that featured multiple shots of vodka. I was jet-lagged, tipsy, and struggling to keep my eyes open when Leida tapped me on the shoulder and asked me to follow her to a small backroom.

After indicating that I should sit on her bed, she took a heavy, metallic bracelet from her jewelry box and placed it on my wrist. I told her I could not possibly accept it, but she firmly grasped my hand, saying, "No, please—it's for you."

Then she my looked directly into eyes and said in a low voice, "Now I have something special to show."

Rummaging through the top drawer of her dresser, she pulled out a small parcel that she cradled as if it were a precious porcelain cup.

"It's from the homeland," she said proudly.

I was stunned to see that she was holding a bag of dirt. Her eyes misted, as she looked through the window into the distance towards Estonia, her native land, that seemed so near yet so impossibly far away. What would it be like, I wondered, to have lost your ability to return to the country that was a part of your identity? How agonizing would it be to know you could never travel back to reclaim the person you once were?

According to historical records, the strong attachment that Estonians have to their land extends back tens of thousands of years. As early as 98 A.D., the Roman historian, Tacitus, noted in his treatise, *Germania*, that Estonian tribes were living along the rocky shores of the Baltic Sea.

After Estonia was conquered by the German Knights in the 13th century, the country was successively occupied by the Germans, the Danes, the Swedes, the Poles, and finally by the Russians. Yet despite centuries of foreign domination,

Estonians clung to their language, their ethnic identity, and their shared cultural heritage. After winning a hard-fought, two-year War of Independence, the country finally became independent in 1918.

At the beginning of World War II, when the Soviets took control over Estonia in 1940, many hoped that Estonia's independence would be restored after the Germans invaded the Soviet Union. Given the terror tens of thousands of Estonians suffered during the Soviet occupation, they cheered when Hitler launched his invasion of the Soviet Union on June 22, 1941.

Joseph Stalin's response was more sinister. As he watched three million German troops quickly advance into the Soviet-occupied areas of Poland,[35] Stalin ordered Soviet officials to implement a scorched earth policy. To assure nothing would remain that could assist the Germans, Destruction Battalions were deputized to burn buildings, destroy crops, kill livestock, and murder those civilians in Estonian towns and villages who stood in their way.[36]

Alarmed at the rapid advance of the German army, Soviet tribunals quickly imposed death sentences on the Estonian political prisoners who were still being detained. In response, Soviet guards killed 199 inmates in Tartu, burying some of the corpses in the courtyard while throwing others into a well. [37]

In Tallinn, the Soviet guards executed Ülo Maramaa and his fellow co-conspirators from the Salvation Committee,

35   "Operation Barbarossa," Wikipedia.

36   "Estonia_in_World_War_II," Wikipedia.

37   Estonian State Commission, "The White Book," 15.

along with other prominent Estonian statesmen and military leaders. Similar prisoner executions took place in Viljandi where Red Army soldiers shot eleven prisoners before retreating. Instead of killing my grandfather's brother, Jakob Vares, the Soviets decided to transport him to Tallinn.

"No one in my family talked about what happened to Jakob," my mother said. "My father told us the Soviets took him away and then, when we did not hear from him again, we assumed he disappeared somewhere in Russia."

Even though my grandfather never shared what he knew, he must have learned his brother's fate. Shortly after their arrival, German officials set out to prove that the Soviets had committed atrocities in Estonia. Among the mass grave sites they uncovered, German troops found more than one hundred decomposing bodies at the summer house of Estonian banker Klaus Scheel in Pirita-Kosel.

The prisoners had their hands tied behind their backs and cloth bindings over their mouths, suggesting they were buried alive. Some of the corpses showed signs of torture including sliced tongues, gauged eyes, and broken bones. Among the deceased, Jakob's body was identified based on the clothing he was wearing.[38] After recovering the bodies of the victims, the Germans shared information regarding the mass executions with Estonian leaders, many of whom were my grandfather's acquaintances.

The news would have been agonizing for my grandfather since my mother always said that he shared a close brotherly bond with Jakob. Born only a year apart, the two supported

---

38   Tamme, "Massacre on Scheel's Plot."

one another throughout their lives. Since my grandfather suffered from a displaced hip from birth, he probably relied on his sturdy younger brother to help with their farm chores.

As they grew older, both brothers traveled to Russia where my grandfather trained as a physician in Moscow while Jakob served in the Tsar's army during World War I. After they returned to Estonia, Jakob and my grandfather married and started families, always living close to one another. When Jakob was looking for a job in law enforcement, it was my grandfather who recommended that he be selected to head the Viljandi police department.

Side-by-side pictures show how closely the brothers resembled one another. In his photo, Jakob wears the hat of a senior military officer while proudly displaying the medals he earned during Estonia's War of Independence, the awards the Soviets likely used to justify his execution. By contrast, my grandfather is dressed in a somber business suit. Yet, both men have the same square jaw line, the same steady gaze, and the same determined expression. They probably believed they would always be together. Jakob was only fifty-two when he was executed. It was a fate that my grandfather could easily have shared.

Jakob Vares

Jaan Vares

While the Soviets were retreating, they issued a broad mobilization order, requiring all able-bodied young men to serve in the Red Army. Those who resisted were executed and their families were arrested.[39] Within a matter of only a few weeks, thirty-three thousand young Estonian men were conscripted to fight alongside the Soviets.[40]

To avoid being deported in the early months of the summer, young Estonians began hiding in the Estonian countryside. Many more disappeared into the woods after the Soviets began drafting Estonian men. Intent on fighting for Estonia's independence, they banded together to sabotage the retreating Soviet soldiers while also defending local towns from the Soviet-sponsored Destruction Battalions.

As the German army advanced toward Estonia, close to ten thousand partisan fighters joined together in an informal network of Home Guard (or Omakaitse) units.[41] All prospective members were required to swear they were not affiliated with any Communist organizations. Bruno, intent on proving his true allegiances as an Estonian patriot, joined the Home Guard unit that was being formed in Tänassilma.

Terror reigned throughout Estonia during the early summer months of 1941 as the Soviet forces retreated and the Destruction Battalions roamed throughout the countryside. Farmers who defended their property were executed while those who supported the Home Guard partisans were tortured and killed. In some communities, the Destruction Battalions

---

39 Larr, *Red Terror*.

40 Röngelep and Clemmesen, "Tartu in 1941."

41 "Guerilla War in the Baltic States," Wikipedia.

forced civilians to build defensive fortifications to strengthen the ability of the Soviet soldiers to hold back the advancing German military.

Near the village of Rani on the outskirts of Tartu, six thousand Estonian citizens were forced to dig an anti-tank trench on the perimeters of the city. Using only picks and shovels, the Estonians dug a deep ravine intended to prevent any German tanks from breaching the defensive line that the Soviet soldiers established around the borders of Tartu.

As the Red Army reinforced its defensive positions, small groups of Estonian partisans disrupted their efforts by cutting telephone lines, setting up roadblocks, and blowing up bridges. Some of the Estonian men who had been conscripted deserted in large numbers and turned their weapons against their Soviet commanders.

To impede the Destruction Battalions, the Home Guard partisans created protective barriers around farms and villages. Yet, despite their efforts, the havoc caused by the Destruction Battalions was widespread as 3,237 Estonian farms were destroyed, 13,500 buildings were burned, and 2,199 civilians were killed.[42]

While the Estonian partisans slowed the carnage caused by the Destruction Battalions, they also achieved some military success. In southern Estonia, Home Guard squadrons recaptured much of the territory that the Soviets abandoned as they retreated toward Russia.[43] Members of the Home Guard also took over the town of Tartu and successfully defended it

---

42   "Estonia in World War II." Wikipedia.

43   Laar, The *Forgotten War*.

against the Red Army for two weeks until the German troops arrived in mid-July.[44]

My mother remembered when the first German troop trucks arrived in Viljandi on July 8. Thrilled by the prospect that the Soviets would soon be gone, she grabbed Asta's arm and together they raced together toward the center of town.

Despite the rumbling of cannon fire in the distance, the two sisters cheered and gathered flowers to welcome the German soldiers when they marched into the town square. Oblivious to any danger they might face, they both laughed as they scrambled beneath a nearby hedge when a squadron of Luftwaffe planes thundered overhead.

"We were crazy to think the bushes were going to protect us," Mom said. "But we were both so deliriously happy because Estonia was finally going to be free."

After reaching the center of town, the sisters discovered that a crowd had already begun gathering to celebrate the long-awaited liberation of Estonia. The people of Viljandi were jubilant, believing once the hated Soviet occupiers were gone, they would be able to regain control over their lives.

On the outskirts of Viljandi, the battle between the German Wehrmacht forces and the Red Army lasted for twelve hours before the Soviets finally retreated. Once the fighting was over, members of the Home Guard herded the Soviet soldiers who had been captured into make-shift prisoner of war camps while Estonian medical teams turned their attention to the large numbers of injured soldiers who required medical attention.

---

44   Laar, Estonia in World War II.

Those with the most severe wounds were taken to a temporary military hospital that was set up in Viljandi's Grand Hotel. When the call went out for medical volunteers, my grandfather and Asta rushed to help triage the injured soldiers and to care for those who had the most serious injuries.

Writing later in her diary, Asta lamented the cruelty of war that left some soldiers mortally wounded while others survived.

> The hospital is filled with the wounded. One sighs, another suffers in silence, and a third speaks of love in an attempt to forget the pain. War—it leaves people barren of tender-heartedness and all but kills compassion. Some soldiers are listening to dance music in one room while their brother-in-arms succumbs to his wounds in the next. Such is life.

Soviet Prisoners of War in front of the
Grand Hotel, the Site of a Military Hospital,
Viljandi, June, 1941 (Viljandi Museum)

While Asta was gratified that Bruno had been able to join an Estonian partisan group in Tänassilma, she recognized there were many people in Viljandi who still blamed him for the atrocities that occurred while the Communist Party was in power, as well as for the damage that was being caused by the Destruction Battalions and the retreating Soviet army.

Before the Soviet soldiers left town, they set fire to the Viljandi bank and the town's match factory.[45] They also stole machinery, cattle, and farm vehicles while leaving behind the bodies of the prisoners who were executed at the Viljandi jail. Given all the suffering Estonians had endured, many of the residents of Viljandi wanted the Party leaders to be held accountable.

To avoid being captured, many of those who had been in charge of the Communist Party in Viljandi escaped to Russia with the Red Army, leaving Bruno as one of the few well-known Party members who remained in town. To Asta's dismay, even Bruno's closest acquaintances began denouncing him and calling for his arrest. In one diary entry, she wrote,

"Some people are fleeing. Others are called traitors by their friends."

Despite the speed with which the German army was advancing towards the Soviet Union, Estonia was the last Baltic territory from which the Soviet forces retreated, as fighting across Estonia's countryside continued until the end of August. When Estonia's capital city of Tallinn was finally

---

45   Hiio, "World War II: Military Operations and Units," 11. and Estonia International Commission, "Phase 1: The Soviet Occupation of Estonia."

liberated on August 28, Estonian troops proudly placed their national flag on top of the country's main government building. Yet, only a few hours later, German troops replaced it with the red Nazi flag with its distinctive black swastika.

Even though the early signs showed that the Germans would be assuming control over Estonia's government, Asta tried to remain optimistic. Bruno had documented why he joined the Communist Party. He had also identified witnesses who would verify how he worked to protect his fellow citizens from being harmed by the Communists. She also expected that Viljandi's civic leaders would vouch for the patriotic sacrifice that Bruno had made at great risk to himself.

The evidence was clear. Yet, Asta also knew that many Estonians wanted revenge against the Communists who had caused the hardship and suffering they experienced over the past year. In some towns, residents were even taking justice into their own hands by executing those Communist officials who remained in Estonia.

Only a few hours after the Soviets retreated, the Estonian police in Viljandi began receiving complaints from residents who asked why well-known Communists such as Bruno were still walking freely through the streets. The police responded quickly, issuing arrest warrants for those who were known to have been associated with the local Communist Party.

Bruno, it turned out, had already been under surveillance by the Viljandi police. In the orders issued for Bruno's arrest, the police noted that Bruno had been observed traveling to Tänassilma. To prevent him from escaping, the local guards were urged to act quickly to take him into custody, since he might be a flight risk.

We have received data that the former Secretary of the Party, Bruno Kulgma Kull, is hiding in the Tänassilma countryside. We know the location of his residence in Viljandi. He is now living with Mayor Hans Miik in Lembert's house. We need to act quickly and set up an arrest dragnet since the Police Department is receiving complaints that Communists are not being arrested. Signed July 29, 1941

After learning that the Estonian police were looking for Bruno, Asta trusted that the town leaders would step forward and explain that her fiancé was an Estonian patriot. Yet even though Bruno had advocates who could attest that he was not a Communist collaborator, the Estonian police needed to be convinced.

CHAPTER 11

BRUNO'S ARREST

While the fighting continued along Estonia's eastern border with Russia, the German authorities established Viljandi as their regional headquarters. Despite Hitler's optimism that the German troops would quickly occupy the Soviet Union, the Wehrmacht forces met fierce Soviet resistance, resulting in heavy casualties on both sides. To support the frontline battalions, the German soldiers based in Estonia travelled throughout the countryside seeking food and other provisions. Those combatants whose wounds were healed were quickly redeployed to the Eastern Front.

After helping the ailing German soldiers regain their strength, Asta worried that they might not survive when they were sent back to their fighting units.

"All the patients have left the hospital, with final handshakes, and farewells. After these people have left my life, will I ever meet any of them again?" she wondered.

Bruno's situation was also uncertain. To support her fiancée, Asta remained in Viljandi to work in her father's office while taking a leave of absence from the University of Tartu. Even though Bruno tried to reassure her, Asta remained apprehensive. Rather than clearing Bruno's name, the Estonian police appeared intent on proving that he had been a high-ranking member of the Communist Party who deserved to be punished for his crimes.

While the Germans were consolidating their control over Estonia, Mom said that few Estonians were aligned with the Nazi Party's political and racial philosophies. Yet, many still considered Germany to be an ally in Estonia's fight against the Soviet Union. Some Estonian young men, in a show of patriotism, even joined the German army, believing this was the best way to assure Estonia could regain its independence in the future.

When three Wehrmacht officers announced their intention to take over one of my grandfather's examination rooms for their living quarters, the Vares family was happy to accommodate them.

"The German officers were always polite and never caused us any trouble," Mom said. "They even arranged for the X-ray machine that the Soviets had appropriated to be returned to my father's office."

Mom never acknowledged that the officers who were living in her family home were part of the German high command, but she must have known they were influential. One of her family's lodgers was Ernst-Wilhelm Keitel, the son of Wilhelm Keitel, Hitler's Chief of the Reich Ministry of War, who commanded Germany's army, navy, and air force. From my mother's perspective, Ernst was merely a quiet young man who greeted her when they met in the front hallway.

After the German authorities allowed the University of Tartu to reopen, Mom was overjoyed to become a first-year medical student, despite her ambivalence about becoming a doctor. Being 20 years old, she rejoiced that she could finally live away from home and she was ready to make the most of this opportunity. Shortly after arriving in Tartu, she filled her photo album with pictures that captured the many parties she enjoyed with large groups of friends, all of whom wanted to forget the war that was being fought only a few hundred miles away.

A short time after she settled into her new apartment, Mom remembered being surprised to find my grandfather knocking at her door to check on how she was adjusting to life as a university student. The party she hosted the night before had been raucous and given my grandfather's surprise visit, Mom did not have time to clear away the debris that littered the floor. Rather than comment on the empty vodka bottles, my grandfather merely encouraged her to focus on her studies. Mom was young and impetuous, but she promised to do better.

In the later part of the summer, Bruno returned from Tänassilma and began hiding in the attic of the Vares family home. Recognizing that he would eventually need to face the Estonian police, he started to compile all the material he needed for his defense while collecting support letters from the town leaders who knew about his efforts to spy on behalf of Estonia.

Even though the Estonian police may have been convinced by Bruno's defenders, they harbored a deep resentment against the Communist Party and those who were associated with the Party's efforts to execute anyone associated with Estonia's military or police force. Their intense antipathy was encouraged by the German officials who urged the local

Estonian police to take a hard line against those who were members of the Communist Party.

Even before Germany launched its invasion, Hitler informed his most senior military officers that he expected them to eradicate all those who were associated with the Communist Party. As Hitler explained, "This is a war of annihilation. The War against Russia [is a war of] extermination of the Bolshevik commissars and of the Communist intelligentsia."

Soon after the Germans began advancing toward the Soviet Union, Reinhard Heydrich echoed Hitler's command and ordered the German officers heading the Einsatzgruppen forces to enforce the strictest measures against suspected Communists, writing, "All officials of the Comintern (and Communist politicians in general), the higher, mid-level and radical low-level officials of the party, of the Central Committee, of the regional committees, people's commissars, Jews employed in party and state functions, other radical elements (saboteurs, propagandists, snipers, assassins, agitators, etc.) have to be executed."[46]

When Martin Sandberger, a 30-year-old Nazi zealot, arrived in Tallinn to take charge of the German Einsatzgruppen forces in Estonia, he was eager to comply. Only two years earlier, Sandberger had distinguished himself to the German High Command when he supervised the deportation of Jews, Poles, and Slovenians from territories the Germans were occupying. In his new post, Sandberger was confident that under his command, he would ensure that all the enemies of

---

46   Burds, "Collaborators, the German Occupation and Stalin's NKVD.".

the Third Reich in Estonia would be eliminated, particularly Jews and Communists.

Compared with the other Baltic countries, Estonia had a relatively small Jewish population. Many of the roughly 4,500 Jews who lived in Estonia at the beginning of the war left the country before the German troops arrived. Roughly five hundred were deported to Siberia during the Soviet occupation, while another three thousand Jews escaped to Russia as the Germans were advancing toward Estonia.[47]

As one of his first orders after arriving in Estonia, Sandberger ordered his German troops to identify and arrest the Jews still living in Estonia. They were criminals, according to Sandberger. Anyone who was Jewish was also a Communist who was acting as a Soviet spy to sabotage the rear lines of the Wehrmacht forces.

As the Germans had done in the other countries they occupied, German officials required that Jews wear a yellow star. They also prohibited Jewish people from walking along the sidewalk, using transportation, or going to theaters, museums, the cinema, or schools. After closing Jewish businesses and confiscating property owned by Jews, the German forces then arrested Jewish business owners and condemned them to death.

To further justify the death sentences given to Jewish prisoners, Sandberger contended that the Jews were part of the global Communist conspiracy and should, therefore, be held responsible for the crimes the Communists committed in Estonia during the Soviet occupation. Within a matter of

---

47   Berger, "Some in Estonia Greeted Nazis in '41 as Liberators."

months, the first executions of Jewish prisoners began taking place.

While my mother was finding her way among the university buildings in Tartu, the German military police started to round up Jews and detain them in the Kuperjanov barracks at the edge of town. A short time after they were arrested, German Field Commandant Fahrnberger, who oversaw the Tartu prison, ordered that all Jewish prisoners should be executed.

On the days when the executions were scheduled to occur, small groups of prisoners were escorted from the barracks and told to strip to their underwear. To prevent the prisoners from trying to escape, the guards tied their hands together with a rope before driving them to the anti-tank trench that the Soviets had forced local townspeople to construct only a few months earlier on the outskirts of town. After the prisoners knelt in front of the trench, the guards lined up behind them and then aimed their rifles as they shot each of the detainees in the head.[48]

While the Nazi Secret Police worked to execute Jewish men, women, and children throughout Estonia, Sandberger urged his troops to be equally vigilant in rounding up all those who had been associated with the Communist Party. Building on the hatred Estonians felt towards the Communists, Sandberger encouraged his Waffen-SS officers to recruit members of the Estonian Home Guard and other Estonian police officers to help carry out the arrests and executions of those the Germans considered to be undesirable.

---

48   Maripuu, "The Execution of Estonian Jews."

Within only a few months, Sandberger was pleased to report to his superiors that the Estonian local police had helped to arrest 620 Bolshevist officials and other Communists. In his progress report, he bragged,

"The Estonians make any effort you can think of to support the Wehrmacht and to show their good will. In tracking down Estonian Bolshevists and taking them to court, they have frequently shown the desired cooperation."[49]

In alignment with Nazi policies, the Estonian police were encouraged to arrest those who had helped the Communists in any type of capacity. Beyond membership in the Party, other offenses that warranted detention included distributing Communist propaganda and the more nebulous charge of sympathizing with the Soviet occupiers.

In his October progress report, Sandberger detailed how well the "self-cleansing" efforts in Estonia were progressing as German authorities took full control over Estonian police operations.

"Generally speaking, the population is used to the fact that the Germans now call the shots in Estonia," he wrote. "All measures taken are being carried through obediently."

Within a matter of months, Sandberger boasted that the Nazi campaign against Estonia's Jewish population was achieving all its goals.[50] In fact, the Nazi commandant predicted that by the end of the year, Estonia would become free of all Jews (or Judenfrie).

---

49   Traces of War, "Martin Sandberger."

50   "History of the Jews in Estonia," Wikipedia.

The arrest of all male Jews of over 16 years of age has been nearly finished. With the exception of the doctors and the elders of the Jews who were appointed by the special Kommandos, they were executed by the self-protection units under the control of the special detachment. Jewesses in Pärnu and Tallinn of the age groups from 16 to 60 who are fit for work were arrested and put to peat-cutting or other labor. At present a camp is being constructed in Harku in which all Estonian Jews are to be assembled so that Estonia will be free of Jews in a short while.[51]

Coupled with Sandberger's aggressive efforts to eliminate Estonia's Jewish population, he also pledged to exterminate those Estonians who had any connection with the Communist Party. Within a matter of months, he gloated that due to his leadership, the Communist threat in Estonia had largely been annihilated.

With the exception of one, all leading Communist officials in Estonia have now been seized and rendered harmless. The sum total of Communists seized runs to about 14,500. Of these about 1,000 prisoners were shot and 5,377 inmates put in concentration camps [while] 3,785 less guilty supporters were released.[52]

---

51 Jewish Virtual Library, "The Einsatzgruppen."
52 "Martin Sandberger," Wikipedia.

Yet, despite this evident progress, Sandberger worried that the Estonian police were not being sufficiently diligent in their efforts to rid the country of anyone who had been aligned with the Communist cause.

As he detailed in a written order that was sent to the German security officers and their Estonian partners, Sandberger reiterated his expectation that all those who were even suspected of being a Communist were to be treated with the harshest of measures without any "sentiments of objectivity and humanitarian considerations."

"Better to lock up ten innocents," Sandberger advised, "than let even one [who is] guilty run free."[53]

Given the incessant pressure from the German authorities to apprehend Communists, the local Estonian police officers in Viljandi redoubled their investigation into Bruno's involvement with the Communist Party.

When Artur Pari, the Assistant Commissioner for the Viljandi Prefecture, was unable to locate Bruno in Tänassilma, he instead interviewed Hans Miik, the town's Mayor, who had once given Bruno a place to stay. As Pari later detailed in a written report, Miik testified that Bruno was a kind and trustworthy person who had helped protect Tänassilma when the town was being attacked by the Soviet Destruction Battalions.

It was Bruno, Miik attested, who only a few months earlier had warned the mayor when he was about to be arrested by the Soviet Secret Police. Because of Bruno's intervention,

---

53 Traces of War, "Martin Sandberger."

Miik escaped into the forest even though he was unable to protect the rest of his family from being deported.

Miik assured Commissioner Pari that Bruno was not a Communist but was instead a young man who joined the Party to earn money. While he did not know Bruno's current location, the Mayor assumed that his former colleague had returned to Viljandi. In his written notes from the interview, Pari later scribbled in the margin that Miik's testimony was believable.

While he was in Tänassilma, Commissioner Pari also interviewed Marie Toha who replaced Bruno as the town's Assistant Municipal Secretary when Bruno joined the Communist Party. Toha testified that Bruno always spoke about the Communist regime with disgust. In January, Bruno told her he wanted to quit the Party, but he expected that he would come under suspicion if he tried to leave. In Toha's opinion, Bruno was not a Communist but rather someone who wanted to use his position in the Party to subvert the Soviet plans to undermine Estonia's institutions.

While Commissioner Pari was conducting his interviews in Tänassilma, Bruno was finishing the last pages of his defense brief and compiling the support letters he believed would substantiate his written testimony. Once he had assembled all the evidence he planned to submit to the Estonian police, Bruno voluntarily arranged to be interviewed by investigators who were working within Viljandi's Criminal and Security Police Division.

Among the material he submitted during his first appearance at the police station, Bruno provided a twenty-five-page typed summary that highlighted the many ways he had helped the residents of Viljandi. He also supplied twelve handwritten support letters from the Mayor of Viljandi, the Mayor of Tänassilma, the Director of Prisons, the head of the county Health Department, and the Hospital Director among others.

One of the attached letters was signed by my grandfather, but the emotion-laden text was clearly written by Asta. In a heartfelt plea, she pointed out that Viljandi's civic leaders knew from the outset why Bruno joined the Communist Party. All the available evidence, she explained, demonstrated that rather than being a Communist, Bruno had done everything in his power to help Estonia. Any blame for the criminal actions that occurred, she argued, should more appropriately be placed on the Communist Party officials who were in fact the ones in control while Estonia was occupied by the Soviets.

Bruno, she pointed out, was forced for his own survival to keep his intentions secret. Even though he authored newspaper articles supporting the Communist Party, she noted there was nothing within the material that in any way undermined the cause of Estonian independence.

In conclusion, she insisted, "Given this true accounting, no one has the right to criticize and punish him."

The other letter writers described Bruno as a patriot who sought to mitigate the terrorist crimes that were committed by the Soviet regime. In their fervent statements, they explained that Bruno ignored any risk to himself when he discredited Communist officials and passed along information regarding Party activities to Estonian leaders. His brave actions, they asserted, helped many local residents to retain their jobs while preventing others from being arrested.

As the Estonian police reviewed the material that Bruno submitted, an investigator from Viljandi's Criminal Security

Division gathered additional information from two other witnesses. A local teacher testified that Bruno warned her when she raised the suspicion of the NKVD because she had relatives in Germany. Following Bruno's advice, she distributed false stories filled with exaggerated praise for the local Communist authorities, a ploy that she believed helped to hide her true allegiances.

When the Viljandi investigators interviewed one of Bruno's fraternity brothers, he confirmed that Bruno was a staunch anti-Communist who plotted with others to sabotage the Soviet take-over of Estonia. Bruno, he said, was part of a network of student activists who intentionally integrated themselves within the Communist hierarchy to thwart, subvert, and block the Soviet regime. The fraternity brothers, the interviewee confirmed, were all patriots who expected the Communist occupation to end once Germany invaded the Soviet Union.

Despite the pressure Commissioner Pari was under from the German officials who supervised Estonia's jails and prison systems, he submitted a handwritten memo in which he concluded that, based on the evidence he had collected, Bruno was innocent of the charges against him.

Statement: In the revision of B. Kulgma's investigation file, it appears that B. Kulgma has joined the party with the knowledge and under the recommendation of a number of well-known members of the town government. His purpose was to contribute to the survival of people of Estonian-minded characters and to report on the activities of the Communist Party. Kulgma has also given the police a list of Party leaders and provided information regarding other Communist figures.

After submitting his final report, Pari asked to be removed from Bruno's case. While he had reached a determination based on the evidence he collected, he knew that the German authorities did not consider his conclusions to be final. Recognizing the political pressure that the Germans were applying, Pari recommended that officers within the Criminal Security Division in the Viljandi Police Prefecture should be assigned to the investigation in the event that additional information needed to be collected.

Investigator Pari may have been convinced that Bruno was innocent but others within the Viljandi Police Prefecture remained suspicious. The Germans expected the Estonian police to assume that anyone who had any connection with the Communist Party was guilty of being a Communist. The police were also hearing complaints from residents of the town who demanded to know why Bruno had not been arrested. In response to the angry questioning, the police ordered Bruno to sequester himself at his uncle's house on the outskirts of Viljandi while they gathered more witness testimony.

During the subsequent police interviews, a fellow ESS fraternity member confirmed that Bruno was a strident anti-Communist who became too entangled within the Party to be able to quit. Once the Soviets retreated from Estonia, the witness asserted that Bruno wanted to be among the first to declare his anti-Communist sentiments.

A former judge provided a different perspective, claiming that Bruno used his authority within the Party to have him fired despite the judge's experience and qualifications. He characterized Bruno as an opportunist who filled the judiciary with his friends from the University of Tartu. If Bruno was a patriot, as he claimed, the judge insisted that the police should find clear evidence that Bruno had in fact shared intelligence information with the town's leaders.

While he was under house arrest on the outskirts of Viljandi, Bruno felt stranded, cut off, and alone, particularly since the terms of his detention had no end date. Knowing that some in town regarded him as a traitor, he was careful to protect Asta's reputation. The couple limited the times they were seen in public and only shared the news of their engagement with their closest friends. Yet when Asta celebrated her twenty-second birthday at the beginning of September, Bruno arranged for a short visit.

Within a day, some neighbors contacted the Viljandi police headquarters, demanding to know why Bruno was still free. In response to their criticism, the police ordered Bruno to appear before a local magistrate. During the hearing, Bruno said that he knew some of the town's residents wanted him to remain under house arrest, but he explained that it was difficult for him to comply with the terms of his confinement.

Since his uncle and his aunt had only a few rooms in their residence, they had no additional space to accommodate him. In addition, the school principal had begun spreading rumors that Bruno's uncle was also a Communist. To protect his uncle, Bruno relocated to an adjacent school building. While he admitted that he left the space on three occasions, he said that he only visited his former apartment to do his laundry.

To quell the continuing complaints, the Viljandi police changed the location of Bruno's house arrest to Tänassilma. Under the new arrest orders, Bruno was told that he could only leave the village after he informed the police. He was also forbidden to talk about his involvement with the Communist Party. Should he disobey any of these restrictions, the police warned Bruno that he could face additional interrogations and more severe punishment.

Being confined in Tänassilma was easier for Bruno than his house arrest in Viljandi. He was acquainted with many of the village residents and had connections with local Home Guard partisans. Asta, on the other hand, believed that Bruno was being banished. She had hoped that Bruno's testimony would prove that he was innocent, but instead of being released, the new terms of her fiancée's house arrest had become even more restrictive. Bruno was not able to travel to Viljandi and since Asta did not have a car, she had few options for visiting him.

At the end of September, while Bruno was settling into Tänassilma, the Eighteenth German Army formally designated Estonia as the staging ground for its continued assault on Leningrad. After the last Red Army brigades retreated from Estonia, the Wehrmacht disbanded Estonia's Home Guard units and reorganized the partisan militias into an auxiliary police force.

After Johannes Soodla, a former Estonian military officer, was appointed to head the Estonian Directorate of the Interior, he issued protocols at the end of September that defined the duties of the local Estonian police departments.[54] Under the new policies, the Estonian police were given responsibility for investigating, arresting, and sentencing prisoners. Once

54 Estonian International Commission, "Phase II: The German Occupation of Estonia.".

their investigations were completed, higher-ranking German officers had the final authority to either endorse or revise the sentences that the Estonian police had recommended.

After the local police departments were restructured, Bruno's case files were transferred from Viljandi to the police prefecture in Tartu, which was located fifty miles to the east. While the Viljandi police had been willing to judge the evidence in Bruno's case favorably, the Tartu authorities moved quickly and issued a warrant for Bruno's arrest, charging him with being a Communist.

On a cloudy Tuesday morning, a police van parked in front of the small, wood-frame house where Bruno was staying in Tänassilma. As a brisk winter wind rustled through the nearby trees, Bruno was handcuffed and transported to the prison in Tartu. The arrest warrant detailed the charges that Bruno was facing. In addition to the crimes that he was alleged to have committed as a Communist, Bruno was accused of being part of a secret network of Communists who remained in Estonia.

> Investigation official at the Prefecture of Tartu, B Fuht, testifies that Bruno Kulgma, a citizen of the Tänassilma, is suspected of being a Communist and other related crimes. His continued freedom is evidence of the pernicious presence of the clandestine regime. On the morning of October 14, Bruno Kulgma has been arrested and is now in custodial cell number 12.15

Despite the extensive evidence that the Viljandi police had compiled that demonstrated that Bruno was an Estonian patriot, the Tartu investigators started with the assumption that Bruno was guilty as charged. The only evidence German

Field Commandant Fahrnberger needed to know was that Bruno was a card-carrying member of the Communist Party who had publicly proclaimed his loyalty to the Party and its ideology. Even if he was working for the Estonian cause and even if he had helped his fellow Estonians, he remained an enemy of the Third Reich.

CHAPTER 12

FLEETING HOPE

After Bruno was taken to the Tartu prison, my mother said her family tried desperately to identify anyone who could help win his release. Having less influence in Tartu, my grandfather along with the other civic leaders in Viljandi struggled to identify those who might have influence with the Tartu prison authorities. Since the Germans discouraged any visits to the Kuperjanov Barracks where Bruno was being held, no one could confirm when a formal review of Bruno's case might be scheduled.

Hoping to advocate for Bruno's innocence, Albert Vilms, Viljandi's Mayor, traveled to Tartu to meet with the Tartu prison officials. Vilms affirmed that Bruno's decision to join the Communist Party was supported by Viljandi's town leaders. Bruno, he explained, had helped the Estonian cause by providing inside information regarding the Party's operations. Through his efforts, Bruno defended Estonians who were under investigation and enabled many of Viljandi's residents to keep their jobs. In Bruno's defense, Vilms pointed to the extensive evidence collected by the Viljandi police investigators that demonstrated how Bruno had tried to sabotage the Soviet takeover schemes. The Tartu prison officials were unmoved.

When he was initially detained in the Tartu prison, Bruno hoped that he might have a speedy trial. He was confident that the evidence he had compiled would prove his innocence. He knew as well that the Viljandi town leaders would testify that he only joined the Communist Party to support the Estonian cause. To further bolster his case, Bruno supplied the police investigators with a lengthy list of other witnesses who could confirm how he had protected many Estonians while also subverting the Soviet occupation plans.

To win over the Tartu prison officials, Bruno set out to be as helpful as possible. During his early interrogations, he reminded the Tartu police that he had already provided the Viljandi investigators with the names of over one hundred people who had been active members of the Communist Party.

Yet, despite the ample evidence pointing to his innocence, Bruno discovered that the Tartu police suspected that he was downplaying his true role within Viljandi's Communist Party. Despite the conclusions reached by the Viljandi police investigators, the Tartu prison officials noted that Bruno was listed as the Chairman of the Viljandi Communist Party in some of the documents they had confiscated. They also found his signature at the bottom of several Party reports.

In addition to this incriminating evidence, the Tartu officials uncovered four newspaper articles on Marxist-Leninist topics that Bruno had authored. They also identified thirteen public events during which Bruno gave speeches promoting the Communist Party. Even though Bruno might deny that he had any influence within the Party, the Tartu police had discovered materials in his file that led them to conclude that Bruno was one of the region's top Communist leaders.

Still wanting to believe that the witness evidence Bruno had compiled would prove his innocence, Asta tried to remain hopeful. From her perspective, Bruno deserved to be recognized as a hero who sacrificed himself to help many people in the town of Viljandi even while he was under surveillance by the Soviet Secret Police. How, she wondered, could he be charged with committing any crimes?

Determined to speak on her fiancée's behalf, Asta travelled to Tartu. Only a few months earlier, the university town had been the site of bitter fighting between the German forces and the retreating Red Army. After the city center was heavily bombarded, Asta hardly recognized the places she had known as a student. Scores of the university's buildings had been demolished, several of the bridges that once spanned the Emajõgi river were gone and most of the city's market square was reduced to rubble.[55]

In hopes of filing a petition for Bruno's release, Asta made her way to the Tartu headquarters of the Waffen SS. The Germans had installed the regional office of the German Secret Service in a four-story, stucco building that featured an expansive circular driveway where scores of jeeps and army transport trucks were parked. Threading her way around the watchful Nazi guards with their red arm bands and black boots, Asta found the office of Lieutenant Helmut Kopp. Steeling herself, she resolved to make the strongest possible

---

55   Röngelep, "Tartu in the 1941 Summer War."

case for Bruno's innocence, but she must also have realized that the odds of securing Bruno's release were not in her favor.

Under the arrest protocols established by the Germans, thousands of Estonians had been detained based only on rumor and innuendo. Bruno, by contrast, was a card-carrying member of the Communist Party who publicly praised Marxist-Leninism in newspaper articles. The evidence against him was damning.

At first, Lieutenant Kopp was polite and assured Asta that the Germans would consider all the available evidence before making a final determination on Bruno's case. He pointed out that many prisoners were claiming to be innocent. How could the Germans be sure, he asked, who was telling the truth?

Perhaps, the Lieutenant hinted, he could expedite Bruno's case. But if he agreed to help, how would Asta be willing to show her gratitude? Asta was shocked and insulted by the not-so-subtle bargain the German officer was suggesting. What kind of justice could Bruno expect when the Nazi officials in charge of deciding whether he was guilty or innocent expected favors before reviewing his case?

Frustrated and indignant, Asta returned to Viljandi, and poured out her disgust in her diary.

> Lieutenant Helmut Kopp – Were you serious, even in part, about anything you said? I suppose you must be affected by the war. Why else would you consider such a proposition? What about your good upbringing? How can you stay faithful to your sweetheart in letters when you know you are saying dishonest things to her?

As the weeks turned into months, Asta could see no sign that Bruno would soon be released. She became despondent. In her diary, she tried to recall the happier days that she once spent with her fiancée and wondered whether they would ever be reunited. In these "sad times of suffering," she wrote, "hundreds of wishes fill my heart."

After spending the last year worrying over Bruno's uncertain position within the Communist Party, she wanted to believe that once the Germans arrived, he would finally be safe, but she found that her worst fears had come true. While Bruno had avoided being arrested by the Soviets, he had instead been taken into custody by Estonians who were acting under orders from the Germans.

While Asta's pessimism grew, my mother stayed convinced that Bruno would eventually be released since she knew he had not committed any crimes. Mom was sure the evidence would prove that Bruno's sole purpose had always been to subvert the Communist Party rather than to support it. Once the prison officials reviewed Bruno's testimony and his letters of support, they would have to conclude that he was not a security risk to the German army, but rather someone who had fought alongside Estonian partisans to force the Red Army to retreat.

As the Christmas season approached, Asta faced a lonely holiday season without her fiancée. A year earlier, they announced their engagement. Now, with Bruno still detained in the Tartu prison, their future together seemed precarious. In the early weeks of December, the Vares family also suffered an additional loss when Tatsu's husband, Eduard, became seriously ill and died.

As she faced the devastating loss of another beloved family member, Asta turned to her diary where she wrote words of comfort for her grandmother.

> Grandfather is dead. Another family member leaves us for good. Tatsu, your sufferings have been great, but so far God has helped you overcome them all. He is likely to give you strength to cope with this pain as well.

To manage her continued fear over Bruno's safety, Asta stayed busy, helping in her father's office. She also spent long hours assisting a German doctor who staffed a rehabilitation clinic in Viljandi. They were friends who were both far apart from the people they loved. They also experienced the same numb grief that came from watching so many of their patients die. While she worried over her fiancée, Asta valued the opportunity to share time with a colleague, writing in her diary,

> That you do not speak to me of love or promises, instead taking it in your stride, as I do. It's nice to sit in the moonlight and feel happy to be together and then wish each other all the best and thank each other for being so friendly as we depart.

Throughout the fall of 1941, Mom remembered that her sister never stopped anguishing over whether Bruno might be killed. When Asta started to lose weight, everyone assumed that she was merely depressed and not sleeping well. No one expected that a healthy, 22-year-old woman could suddenly become terminally ill.

Years later, Mom recalled the only clue that explained Asta's illness was a dark mole that began festering on her back. After my grandfather insisted that it be removed, the wound refused to heal and small lumps began appearing under Asta's arm. The symptoms were a sign that melanoma, an aggressive form of skin cancer, had begun to metastasize.

Asta was despondent. Despite her efforts, Bruno remained imprisoned. Without having an opportunity to visit him, she could not know how well her fiancée was being treated. She ached to hear his voice and tried to remain hopeful that one day they would again be together. Citing the words of Anna Haava, she grieved over her memories of what used to be, writing,

> Oh, the summer has passed. Only memories remain
> And whispers of love now nothing but an echo
> Like the withered scent of yesterday's roses.

As the winter days grew darker, Asta's expectation that Bruno would be found innocent dimmed along with the shrinking daylight hours. Just as she was losing hope, Asta learned that a neighbor's son, a friend from high school, was working as a guard at the Tartu prison. During one of his weekend leaves, he agreed to meet her one afternoon to share what he knew about the living conditions at the jail.

Bruno, he explained, was not being mistreated. The German SS officers and the Tartu police investigators were using him to gather information about other possible Communist collaborators. So long as he continued to be a useful witness, Bruno was unlikely to be moved to the Death Barracks where those destined to be executed were segregated.

Since Bruno was often escorted to the interrogation rooms, the guard assured Asta he could give him a message, particularly if it was easy to conceal. Thrilled at the opportunity, Asta quickly composed a short note on a folded piece of paper. Trying to give her fiancée hope, she wrote that the family was still working on his behalf. She also told him that she loved him, missed him, and was confident that one day they would be reunited.

To provide Bruno with a chance to respond, Asta handed her palm-sized diary to the guard, explaining that Bruno would know it was hers. After he returned to the Tartu prison, the guard shared Asta's note with Bruno and passed along her diary with a pencil. The next time the two encountered each other, Bruno surreptitiously handed back the diary which the guard then hid in his uniform.

A few days later, when the guard returned to Viljandi, Asta was delighted to see that Bruno had scribbled a note in the back of her diary. With his characteristic humor, Bruno pretended to be a less-than-satisfied guest at a less-than-accommodating hotel.

Hotel Schnapphaus
Asta, my soul, my consolation!
I remain in this pitiful guestroom as a refugee,
where the windows are boarded up with cardboard.
I sit all the time under a quilt with sad thoughts going through my head.
But I am resigned that another chapter of my life has gone by.

Although I cannot be certain about the final resolution, I
am happy that it has passed.

The future is indeed dark but hope still lives.

Despite his grim circumstances, Bruno reassured Asta that
she was still very much in his thoughts. His message consoled
her and led her to believe that if he could be optimistic about
the future, perhaps she should be as well. She clung to his
last words, wanting to trust his vision for a future where hope
could still be alive.

Even though Bruno wrote a positive message to Asta,
he must have been discouraged that there was no sign that
his case would soon be resolved. From his dark prison cell,
only a few hours of daylight broke through the cardboard that
covered his window, otherwise leaving the space around him
filled with inky black shadows. Shivering, when the winter
weather caused the outside temperatures to drop, Bruno clung
to his thin quilt to stay warm. Like Asta, he had hoped that he
might quickly be found innocent, but after spending endless
hours in his cell, Bruno likely began to lose track of time.

For months, he had worn the same clothes, a grey flannel
suit and a white dress shirt that dulled to a grey patina. An
unfamiliar black beard scratched his face, and he could not
remember the last time he combed his hair. After weeks of
captivity, the rancid smells emanating from the barracks no
longer bothered him.

On the occasions when Bruno pondered his fate, he
reasoned that even if he were to be found guilty, membership
in the Communist Party would surely only be a minor charge
that warranted at most a prison term at a labor camp. Based on

the defense materials he had provided as well as the assistance he continued to offer to the police investigators, he must have hoped that whatever sentence he might receive would be minimal.

In some future time, Bruno knew the war would end. While he accepted the fact that he might be sentenced to serve some years in a prison camp, he expected that he would eventually be able to return home to begin a new life with Asta by his side. She would always be his reason for living.

While Bruno dreamed about the future, Asta's health was taking a dire turn for the worse. Mom remembered how shocked she was when she returned home from the university to celebrate the Christmas holidays and saw how thin and weak her once lively sister had become. In addition to having a thick bandage around her back, Asta had a lump under her arm that was almost the size of another breast. She spent much of her time sleeping and had little appetite.

Mom knew how distracted and dejected Asta had become after Bruno was taken to the Tartu prison. Outwardly, Asta kept repeating that she was sure that Bruno would be able to defend himself. The facts, she insisted, were the facts. No one who knew Bruno could believe that he was a Communist traitor. Yet, despite Asta's protests, Mom recognized that if the evidence supporting Bruno's innocence was that obvious, he would have been released months earlier. The longer he was detained, the more at risk he appeared to be, particularly given the rumors that were circulating about the mass executions the Germans had ordered.

The Christmas holidays were somber. Asta tried to join the family, but on most days, she had little strength and preferred to stay in bed. As he watched his oldest daughter grow weaker, my grandfather would have been alarmed. Rather than regaining her strength, he could see that Asta was becoming more bedbound every day. While he changed the bandage on her back, he must also have noticed that instead of healing, the aggressive lesions were spreading and becoming more virulent.

A few days after the family celebrated Christmas, my grandfather finally acknowledged that Asta needed the constant care she could receive at the local hospital that was only six blocks away from the family's house. Although my grandmother wanted to keep Asta at home, she relented after recognizing that Asta needed more care than she was able to provide.

After Asta was admitted, the hospital employees who knew her were shocked by the changes in her appearance. The nurses found it hard to believe that the tireless volunteer who once worked at the military infirmary had become so listless and emaciated. No one could have expected that an otherwise healthy 22-year-old woman would become so seriously ill within the span of a few short months.

Worried that Asta would find herself alone and isolated at the hospital, my grandmother arranged a visit schedule. When it was her turn, Mom recalled spending long afternoons reading out loud to her sister. Setting aside the warm sisterly conversations she had hoped to have, Mom focused instead on trying to make Asta comfortable in her sparse, antiseptic hospital room. Even though Asta insisted she was not feeling any pain, Mom winced as she noticed how the taut, thick bandage that covered Asta's back restricted her sister's movements.

Over the next several weeks, Asta's daily schedule followed a predictable routine. As my grandmother and mother took their respective turns visiting Asta in the afternoon, they watched anxiously to see if Asta's appetite was returning. Even though she told them not to worry, they could both see that Asta's frail body was becoming thinner under the crisp hospital sheets.

As she grew weaker, Asta did not complain about her condition, but rather worried over how she could let Bruno know what was happening to her. If she did not recover, Asta asked my mother to arrange a visit to the Tartu prison to tell Bruno everything Asta was unable to say.

Bruno should know how much she loved him and believed in him. He needed to be told that the family was continuing to work for his release. Even though the future may appear to be dark, she wanted him to always remember that hope still lives.

CHAPTER 13

SEARCHING FOR TRAITORS

My mother recalled 1941 as a year of waiting, worrying, and wondering whether the war would ever end. Coupled with record setting cold temperatures, her future seemed bleak as a dark shadow of war shrouded the globe. After the Japanese bombed Pearl Harbor, the United States declared war on Japan, causing Germany and Italy to declare war on the United States. Even though the places where soldiers were fighting and dying had spread to new battlefronts, Mom hoped that the entry of the American troops would bring the war in Europe to a quick conclusion.

Along the Eastern Front, the news was grim as millions of Soviet and German soldiers continued to lose their lives.[56] Despite the fact that the forward momentum of the German army had stalled, Hitler refused to allow his troops to retreat. Facing subzero temperatures, the vaunted German military

---

56   National WWII Museum, "Operation Barbarossa."

struggled as its aircraft, tanks, artillery, and mechanized vehicles froze in place. Yet, the fighting continued.

After Asta was hospitalized, Mom wanted to believe that her sister would soon begin showing signs of improvement, but as the weeks went by, Asta only grew weaker. Besides worrying about her sister, my mother was also frustrated that Bruno remained imprisoned. Nothing her family had done had made a difference and there was no word as to when Bruno might receive a hearing. Mom could not have known how intent the German high command was to eradicate those Estonians they judged to be undesirable, untrustworthy, and expendable.

Throughout the early months of 1942, Martin Sandberger continued to brag to his superiors that his Einsatzgruppen troops would soon eliminate all Jews, Communists, and other enemies of the Third Reich from Estonia. When he was confronted during his Nuremberg trial regarding the harsh sentences that were given to Jews and Communists, Sandberger claimed that he was only following orders from his superior officer, Bruno Strekenbach. If he had not obeyed the orders that he received to sentence Estonian prisoners to death, Sandberger contended that he himself would have been a martyr.[57]

As part of Sandberger's Nuremberg defense, his attorney, Dr. Bolko von Stein, argued that the Nazi commandant always assured that proper legal proceedings were followed before any prisoners received a death sentence. Stein also asserted that Sandberger made sure that all prisoners were given an

---

57 "Martin Sandberger," Wikipedia.

opportunity to testify in their own defense before they were found guilty.

> When Communist functionaries were executed in the area under [Sandberger's] command or his responsibility, it did not happen in the form of executions but only when guilt had been ascertained in legal procedures and after the person arrested had been granted the opportunity to defend himself during these proceedings.[58]

Yet, despite Sandberger's postwar assertions, the record shows that Bruno never received an impartial court hearing. Within the Tartu prison, sentences were handed down by a military tribunal that included two Estonian officers from the political police and one member of the criminal police unit. As part of their deliberations, the tribunals did not conduct any trial proceedings. Nor were prisoners given an opportunity to testify in their own defense. Instead of allowing prisoners to represent themselves, the tribunals used the case files prepared by the Estonian investigators to decide what they considered to be appropriate verdicts. In some cases, long lists of detainees were automatically given death sentences based on orders from the German authorities.

Even though the tribunals appeared to have some degree of independence, their final decisions were subject to approval by the German field officers. According to historical records, the German Commandant Fahrnberger who oversaw the Tartu prison was well known to impose harsher punishments

---

58   Traces of War, "Martin Sandberger."

than those recommended by the members of the Estonian tribunal.[59]

Despite the odds against him, Bruno was initially hopeful that based on the material compiled by the Viljandi police investigators, the Tartu prison officials would recognize that he was an Estonian loyalist. Yet soon after his arrest, Bruno came to realize that instead the investigators were determined to prove that he was a Communist collaborator.

During one early interrogation, the Tartu officials pointed out that Bruno was a card-carrying member of the Communist Party. They also noted that he had given public speeches and authored newspaper articles that proved his Communist sympathies. As they sought to confirm that Bruno was a long-standing member of the Communist Party, the Tartu officials demanded to know when he was first indoctrinated into Marxist-Leninist teachings.

Wanting to give an honest response, Bruno explained that he developed a superficial understanding of Communist economic theory from a course that he attended in 1937. When the prison officials asked him to identify the Communist who taught the course, Bruno replied that his instructor was Professor Kurtsinski and added that his teacher had since died.

Convinced that Bruno was hiding his true loyalties, the prison officials questioned why Bruno, who claimed to be so eager to help the Estonian people, had not done more to protect those Estonians who were killed by the Communists. Where was he when the Communists ordered tens of thousands of Estonians to be deported and what, if anything, had he done to

---

59   Birn, "Collaboration with Nazi Germany in Eastern Europe."

prevent the chaos caused by the Soviet sponsored Destruction Battalions?

Bruno replied that he had already given the Viljandi police a lengthy, written statement in which he described how he tried to help local Estonians while he was a member of the Communist Party. If that statement was insufficient, Bruno volunteered to explain in more detail how the Communist Party in Viljandi functioned while explaining what his own role had been within the Party.

After the Tartu investigators provided him with paper and a pencil, Bruno returned to his cell and filled thirteen pages with hand-written text. His writing was shaky as he scribbled in his dark cell. He knew that the stakes were high since he could tell that the Tartu prison officials had already decided that he was guilty of being a Communist, independent of whatever his motivations for joining the Party might have been.

As he sketched out the organizational hierarchy of Viljandi's Communist Party, Bruno explained that five members of an Executive Committee (whose names he listed) controlled the Party apparatus. The most important decisions were made by a Russian Communist named Murisepp who received his instructions from Moscow.

Bruno acknowledged that he was selected to serve as the Party's Secretary and was later named to be the titular head of the Party Cabinet, but these positions, he argued, were merely honorific. As he explained in his written testimony,

"At the time the Communists came to power, I did not take part in any meetings or discussions, and I absolutely did not participate in any decision-making. While I was in the Party, I had no knowledge of Estonian Communist Party secrets, but rather just a general understanding of the issues as they were discussed in local newspapers."

Bruno insisted that the leaders of the Communist Party had no authority or influence over the Soviet Secret Police, who were for the most part ethnic Russians who communicated directly with their superiors in Moscow without informing the Party leaders of their plans. As an example, Bruno noted that when the NKVD replaced the attorneys within the Viljandi Prosecutor's Office, they did so without giving the Party officials any advance warning.

Rather than involve themselves in the Party's activities, the Soviet Secret Police relied on the Party leaders to administer the nomination process by which Estonians became members of the Communist Party. Bruno could recall only a few instances when the Soviet Secret Police demanded that certain individuals should be dismissed from the Party based on their alleged disloyalty to the Soviet occupation.

Within his written testimony, Bruno listed the names of fifty Estonians who were avid Party members. He also identified twenty-five Estonians whom he suspected were coerced into working for the NKVD. According to Bruno, those who refused to cooperate with the Soviet Secret Police faced dire consequences. Bruno knew of at least two Viljandi residents who were deported to Siberia after they refused to become informants for the Soviets.

In addition to being independent from the Soviet Secret Police, Bruno explained that the Communist Party officials had little authority or oversight regarding the decisions that were made by the Soviet army. Like the Soviet Secret Police, the Soviet military worked independently from the Party leaders. Bruno pointed out that when the Soviet military decided to place trustworthy Communists in key positions within the police department, they did so without asking for any Party input.

After explaining the distinct spheres of influence in which the Communist Party, the Soviet Secret Police, and the Red Army operated, Bruno described his own role within the Party organization. When he became the Party Secretary, Bruno explained that his main responsibility involved recommending who could join the Party. By being able to influence these decisions, he could also determine which Estonians could remain at their jobs.

Using the influence he acquired as Party Secretary, Bruno described how he assured that local Estonians retained their positions within Viljandi's government, schools, courts, hospitals, and commercial businesses. As Party Secretary, Bruno stated that he was also able to defend those Estonians who were accused by the Soviet Secret Police of having counter-revolutionary views. When Party leaders claimed that the teachers within the local school system were untrustworthy, Bruno spoke in their defense. He also advocated for the Estonian judges who headed the regional courts and protected the Estonian doctors who worked at the town hospital.

The Communist Party officials, according to Bruno, had no direct involvement in the campaign to deport Estonian citizens and were, in fact, caught off guard when the arrests occurred. As proof that the Party leaders had no advance warning regarding those who were going to be deported, Bruno pointed out that to the dismay of Party officials some Party loyalists were among those who were transported to Siberia.

Relative to the Destruction Battalions, Bruno explained that the Soviets recruited Party loyalists, members from Communist youth organizations, and labor camp detainees to implement Stalin's scorched earth policies. When the call for volunteers was issued, Bruno noted that he instead chose to join the partisan Home Guard fighters who were defending the town of Tänassilma against the retreating Red Army soldiers.

Compared with the carefully worded type-written statement that Bruno submitted when he was first arrested in Viljandi, the handwritten defense brief Bruno submitted to the Tartu prison officials was hurried and terse. To avoid being accused of the many crimes that were committed during the Soviet occupation, Bruno tried to provide convincing evidence that the Communist Party leaders operated independently from the Soviet Secret Police and the Red Army officials.

Moreover, Bruno testified that his own role within the Party had been very circumscribed. While he admitted that he acted as the Party's public spokesman, he explained that he was forced to take on this role after he was placed under surveillance by the NKVD. Whatever public pronouncements he made, whether through speeches or newspaper articles, Bruno argued, should be balanced against his many efforts to protect his fellow Estonians and to enable them to retain their jobs.

In conclusion, Bruno offered to provide a list of witnesses who could verify the truthfulness of his statements. He also volunteered to assist the Tartu prison officials in their continuing efforts to arrest those who were true Communist sympathizers. Even though Bruno recognized that the Tartu prison officials believed that he was a Communist insider, he hoped he could convince them that there was a difference between the Estonians who truly supported the Communist Party versus those who were compelled to become Party members to keep their jobs.

Through his written testimony and ongoing interrogations, Bruno hoped that the Tartu prison officials would believe that he was innocent of the charges against him. Yet, he must have despaired as he watched busloads of prisoners being escorted to what was rumored to be the death barracks. As the Kuperjanov Barracks slowly emptied, the inmates whispered that mass executions appeared to be taking place.

The prisoners came to expect that following the nights when they were kept awake by the raucous sounds coming from the drunken guards, a predictable routine would occur on the next day. In the early morning hours, after the guards assembled in front of the barracks, a senior officer would call out the names of a dozen or more prisoners. Once the prisoners entered the courtyard, they were forced to strip to their underwear before being escorted onto a bus that was waiting nearby.

Those prisoners who watched from their windows knew their fellow inmates would never return. They also recognized that at some unknown time in the future they too might be included in the next group that was called into the courtyard.

At the start of 1942, Bruno tried to be optimistic that his possible trip into the courtyard might be postponed since the Tartu prison officials were continuing to use him as an expert witness. Several times during the month of January, Bruno was escorted into an interrogation room where he was asked to confirm whether an Estonian detainee had been a member of the Communist Party.

Bruno tried to be helpful, but in most instances, he testified that he did not know the Estonian prisoners who were accused of having Communist connections. In one instance, Bruno recognized an Estonian who once tried to join the Party, but Bruno explained that the man's application was rejected because of his criminal record. Relative to another prisoner, Bruno recalled that Party officials discussed whether he should be recruited because of his position in a labor union, but the prisoner never applied to become a Party member.

As they tried to take advantage of Bruno's connections, the Tartu prison officials asked him to provide additional information regarding the Communist Party operations in other parts of Estonia. In response, Bruno explained that he was only familiar with the Party activities in Viljandi County. To assist the investigations, Bruno offered to connect the prison officials with a contact in Tallinn who could provide insight into the Party activities in Estonia's capital city even though this individual was not himself a Communist.

While Bruno continued to assist the Tartu prison officials in their investigations into the Communist Party, he could see that by doing so he was putting another nail in his coffin by reinforcing his reputation as a Communist Party insider. Independent of how convincing his defense might be, Bruno recognized that the Tartu prison officials were building a case against him. Since most of Estonia's top Communist Party leaders had fled to Russia, he had become a convenient substitute for those who could no longer be prosecuted. He was also an easy target for the anger and rage many Estonians felt toward the Soviet occupiers.

Even though the Tartu prison officials appreciated Bruno's helpfulness, they were at the same time being pressured by the German authorities to show that they were expeditiously ridding Estonia of all those who had been associated with the Communists. In December, Hitler issued his Night and Fog Decree in which he ordered that all political persons who were hostile to Germany should be sentenced to death without mercy or consideration of international law.[60] In Estonia, Martin Sandberger echoed the same message.

To substantiate their belief that Bruno was an opportunist who took advantage of his position within the Communist Party, the Tartu prison officials questioned his ulterior motives. During one interrogation, they asked Bruno to explain why he had shown favoritism toward Dr. Jaan Vares, his future father-in-law. Bruno admitted that he once destroyed a letter in which a local Communist overheard patients expressing negative views against Communism while they were in Dr. Vares's waiting room. After informing Dr. Vares about the nature of the complaint, Bruno confessed that he destroyed the letter rather than sharing it with other Party officials.

The Tartu investigators remained unconvinced. If he was indeed working on behalf of the Estonian people, why, they wondered, had Bruno chosen to use his influence within the Communist Party to promote only those lawyers he knew from the university. In response, Bruno explained that judicial candidates were approved after their applications were reviewed by several Communist Party committees. Before they were selected, applicants also needed to be vetted by the Soviet Secret Police. As the head of the Nominating Committee, Bruno explained that he could recommend applicants, but he

---

60   "Nacht und Nebel," Wikipedia.

had no control over the final decisions regarding those who would be chosen for certain positions which were under the purview of higher-ranking Communist officials.

The Tartu prison officials continued to question Bruno's motives. While there was evidence that Bruno used his position within the Communist Party to help many Estonians to keep their jobs, the Tartu officials also concluded that Bruno preferentially recommended fellow members of his ESS fraternity for important posts. In conclusion, the lead Tartu prison investigator wrote,

> One gets the impression that Kulgma joined the Communist Party partly for the purpose of spying, but also to promote his own circle of acquaintances. It seems undeniable that Kulgma enabled many Estonian intellectuals to retain their positions, but he also appears to have been biased to some extent. He exercised his power to advance his close associates, while leaving others aside. In this regard, one cannot fail to mention the long-standing hostility and struggle between the student fraternities which is evident in Kulgma's activities.

As they wrapped up their investigation, the Tartu prison officials identified other parts of Bruno's testimony that they considered to be suspicious. While Bruno alleged that he was only the Party's Secretary, the officials uncovered several incriminating documents that identified Bruno as the Chairman of the Party Cabinet. While Bruno could claim that this position had no real authority, the Tartu investigators questioned why he appeared to have approved several Party documents with his signature.

Relative to Bruno's contention that he was under surveillance by the Soviet Secret Police, the Tartu officials could find no evidence that he was forced to write newspaper articles or to give public lectures. Whatever his motivation might have been, the Tartu officials concluded that the fact remained: Bruno was a card-carrying member of the Communist Party who promoted Communist ideology through newspaper articles and public speeches. Other detainees had been executed for far less serious crimes.

As Tartu prison officials continued their interrogations, Bruno became discouraged. When he joined the Communist Party, he had idealistic ambitions to defend his country while thwarting the Soviet occupation. After months of imprisonment, he must have wondered what, if anything, he had accomplished? What difference had he made in the lives of those Estonians he tried to help? What was the point of his sacrifice if even the Tartu prison officials remained unconvinced that he was a true Estonian patriot?

In Viljandi, the Estonian police were inclined to believe that Bruno's defense materials were convincing and trustworthy. They knew the civic leaders who vouched for Bruno and were acquainted with the witnesses who confirmed that Bruno had been a member of various resistance networks. Yet, the Tartu prison officials remained suspicious.

As they concluded their investigation, the prison officials allowed Bruno to read the final police report that they had prepared. After reviewing their conclusions, Bruno became frustrated to see that despite his hours of testimony and his written statements, the Tartu prison officials were continuing to misrepresent him as a Communist sympathizer.

For the record, Bruno corrected the statement that identified him as a life-long Communist, noting that he only joined the Communist Party after he was recruited in the summer of 1940. Bruno also revised the section of the report that characterized him as a decision-maker within the Communist Party, stating that he never participated in any secret Party deliberations. In particular, he specified that he had not been privy to any of the Soviet plans to collectivize privately owned farms.

As a last request, Bruno asked the Tartu investigators to contact the witnesses who could speak on his behalf including many of Viljandi's prominent civic leaders. The investigators might doubt Bruno's testimony, but Bruno asserted that there were others in Viljandi who could confirm that he had been a Communist in name only and should not be held responsible for the criminal acts that occurred during the Soviet occupation.

In conclusion, Bruno testified, "It was always my intention to escape from the Communists and I did so on July 3, 1941, after the arrest and death of one of my close colleagues. I have tried to correct the mistakes in the charges against me. Beyond the testimony I have provided, I can offer no further explanations."

After they finished their final report, the Tartu prison officials forwarded it to the Estonian tribunal for review. The report was also translated into German for approval by Commandant Fahrnberger. All Bruno could do was to wait and hope as he wondered when his case might finally be resolved and what the outcome might be.

CHAPTER 14

LOSING ASTA

At the start of 1942, my mother returned to the University of Tartu to continue her studies, but she came back to Viljandi on the weekends to visit Asta in the hospital, always watching to see if her sister was getting stronger. Even though Asta was mentally alert when she was first admitted, Mom was dismayed to discover that, as the weeks went by, she would often find that her sister stayed asleep while she visited.

During her first semester at the University of Tartu, Mom had only completed the foundational courses for her training as a doctor. She had no ability to diagnose the ways in which her sister's condition was worsening, but she could see that the disease from which Asta was suffering was taking control over her body.

For hours on end, Mom watched as Asta's eyelids fluttered while she drifted in and out of consciousness. Sometimes she could hear Asta sigh, but more often it was only the sound of her sister's heavy breathing that let my mother know that her sister was still alive.

Mom remembered that she felt numb as she watched Asta's health decline. She refused to believe that her beloved sister, her confidant, and her most faithful companion could ever die. Only a year earlier, the two sisters had shared the same bedroom and commiserated with each other as they struggled through the Soviet occupation.

Like many Estonians, they wanted to believe their lives would return to normal once the Germans arrived. After the Soviet threat was gone, they expected their worries for the future would disappear. Their family would be secure, and Bruno would be vindicated when he could finally reveal his true loyalties. Yet, after only a few months into the German occupation, nothing seemed sure anymore.

What might have happened, Mom wondered, if Bruno had not decided to join the Communist Party? Would he still have become a Party member if he had been aware of the risks he was taking? Could he have ever imagined that after being arrested, he would be unable to prove that he was trying to defend his country? Recognizing that Bruno was deeply patriotic, Mom believed that he would have found a way to fight for Estonia, independent of the risks involved. His decision to defend his country was one, she also knew, that Asta supported.

As Mom pondered her what-if questions, she blamed the Soviets for their decision to invade Estonia. How could a stronger neighbor, like the U.S.S.R., have the right to invade a smaller, sovereign nation? If the war had not happened, Bruno would not have chosen to put himself at risk. Perhaps, as well, under a different set of circumstances, Asta might not have become deathly ill.

While Mom tried to make sense of Asta's declining health, my grandfather remained clinically objective. He could see that not only was Asta growing weaker, but after she stopped eating and drinking, he was forced to admit that his first-born daughter would soon be gone. As Asta's last days drew near, my grandfather kept a vigil in her hospital room, sitting beside her bed in a low chair with his head bowed over his cane.

Even though he had witnessed many people die, he had never lost someone who was part of the very fabric of his life. Asta had given him happiness, pride, and hope for the future. When she became terminally ill, she became the source of his deepest sorrow.

While my grandmother could also see that Asta was dying, she tried by the force of her will to bring her back to health. As she sat next to Asta's bed, she clung to her daughter's hands as if she could stop the fatal progression of the disease that was killing her first born child.

After Asta took her last breath on February 19, 1942, the family brought her body home in a wooden coffin. For the next several days before her funeral, Asta's lifeless corpse lay in quiet repose in the family's dining room surrounded by fir sprigs and candles, as family members took turns saying their final farewells.

To deal with her grief, my grandmother busied herself with the arrangements for Asta's funeral and burial. Shortly after Asta's death notice was published, neighbors and friends sent sympathy cards while others printed notes of condolence in the local newspaper. In one posting, Asta's friends from medical school mourned her passing, writing that her memory should not be forgotten during these hard times. In a separate notice, Asta was memorialized by her high school classmates as a beloved alumna who left this life at too early an age.

To ensure that she could frequently visit Asta's grave, my grandmother arranged for her daughter to be buried in a nearby cemetery, selecting a single burial plot that overlooked the town of Viljandi. As a grave marker, she chose a flat, granite tombstone that simply recorded when Asta had been born and when she died. As soon as the weather improved, my grandmother anticipated that she would cover Asta's grave with a blanket of perennial shrubs.

On the day Asta was buried, a small gathering of friends, neighbors, and relatives gathered at the Vares home where a Lutheran minister conducted the funeral. As detailed in a card that commemorated the service, he called on Jesus to heal the family's grief and prayed that Asta would find peace and happiness in her eternal resting place. While acknowledging that Asta's death was untimely, the minister beseeched the family to find consolation in the thought that Asta was in the company of angels. He also asked God to heal their sorrow and to help them to find happiness once again.

While the family may have lost their bright hope for the future, the minister encouraged them to imagine that they were covering Asta's soul with a gentle blanket, as if they were burying a tender plant. Even though Asta may be gone, the minister reassured them that her Eternal Creator was cradling her in love. The family, he said, could find peace and consolation by recognizing the will of God and by praising his angels.

Once the service was over, family members carried Asta's coffin to a horse-drawn sleigh waiting in front of the family's house. The weather was overcast and cold. As my mother huddled with her family in an adjacent sleigh, she remembered the sharp, clacking sound of the hooves of the horses that echoed across the icy, cobblestone streets.

When the funeral procession arrived at the cemetery, family members carried Asta's coffin up a gravel hill to her gravesite, where a gaping hole, surrounded by mounds of freshly shoveled dirt, awaited. Once the mourners convened around the site, several nearby gravediggers helped to lower Asta's body into the empty plot.

After observing a moment of silence, each of the family members threw a handful of dirt on the coffin. As the pellets struck the wooden cover, Mom was forced to confront the fact that her sister was truly gone. Overwhelmed by a crushing sense of loneliness and despair, she resolved to bury her sister's memory deep within her heart while moving forward with her life.

The picture of Asta's gravesite in Viljandi
that my grandmother preserved

My grandfather, by contrast, never recovered from Asta's death. Outwardly he appeared resolute and resigned, but he remained forever haunted by the missing presence of his beloved daughter. As a physician, he felt frustrated that he was unable to stop the disease that took her life. As a father, he ached when he remembered the energetic young woman who always thought more about others than herself: the daughter who was gone and would never return.

After the funeral, my grandmother began the painful task of sorting through Asta's clothes and belongings. Since my mother was living in Tartu, she arranged for my uncle to take over the bedroom that her two daughters once shared. After she stripped the space of anything that would remind her of Asta's death, she collected the memories she wanted to preserve from her daughter's life in a small photo album.

While the Vares family was gathering in Viljandi for Asta's funeral, the prison officials in Tartu were finishing their investigation into Bruno's affiliation with the Communist Party. Under pressure from the German authorities, the Estonian tribunals across the country were accelerating their efforts to empty the prisons. While some political prisoners were sent to labor camps, the tribunals convicted more than six thousand Estonians of being Communist collaborators and sentenced them to death by a firing squad.[61]

While Bruno's fate was still being decided, my mother set out to fulfill the promise she made to Asta that she would visit her fiancé at the Tartu prison. When she submitted her request for a face-to-face meeting, she recognized one of the

---

61   The Baltic Times, "Nazi War Crimes in Estonia."

Estonian guards who was a neighbor from Viljandi. After she explained that Bruno's fiancée had died, the guard agreed to secure the requisite permission that would allow her to meet with Bruno. A few days later, she received a letter stating when her meeting had been scheduled.

On the appointed day, Mom was nervous. She had difficulty talking about Asta's death and knew that Bruno would be devastated when he heard that his fiancée was dead. While she waited for Bruno to arrive, she worried about what she should say. She wanted to honor the promise she made to Asta but also believed that nothing would soften the news that Asta was gone.

When Bruno first entered the room, his face lit up with a happy smile. He was surprised and delighted to see that he had a friendly visitor who could share the latest news from home. After being imprisoned for five months, he was pale, and his eyes were tired, but he eagerly took a seat across from my mother at the small metal table that filled the room.

My mother noticed that Bruno was thinner and had grown a thick beard. She could also see that he was still dressed in the familiar suit jacket and trousers that he was wearing when he was first arrested. After a few minutes of silence, Mom, not knowing how to break the news regarding her sister's death, simply blurted out, "Asta is dead."

Stunned and disbelieving, Bruno was speechless. Mom watched, as his face filled with grief while he searched for an explanation. How could a healthy young woman suddenly die? Not wanting to believe what he had heard, he asked how it had happened.

My mother merely shrugged her shoulders and said, "No one can explain it. Asta just became very sick and then she died."

The two faced each other without speaking as they both struggled to make sense of the improbable news that the woman whom they both knew and loved was gone. Mom wanted to comfort Bruno, but they were sitting across from one another with a table between them while a guard watched from the doorway.

Struggling to stay composed, Bruno got up from his chair and told the guard that he wanted to leave. My mother did not try to stop him. Having shared the news of Asta's death, she found herself reliving once again how her sister had become ill and died. Filled with pain and grief, Mom made her way through the hallway to the main door that led outside the prison. She felt helpless. Her sister was gone and even though her family had done everything possible to free Bruno, he remained a prisoner. As she walked away from the prison, my mother believed that just as she had lost her sister, she would also never see Bruno again.

The news of Asta's death would have overwhelmed Bruno. After losing both of his parents, Asta was the most important person in his life and now she was gone along with the promise of a life Bruno hoped they might share together.

At twenty-seven, he was alone in the world with few hopes for the future. Despite the years he had spent working his way through law school, he found himself imprisoned under the false charge of being a Communist sympathizer and a traitor.

Bruno knew that he was innocent, but from the perspective of those who controlled his fate he was not only a card-carrying Communist, but also someone who was publicly known to have been a member of the Party's leadership circle. Despite all the evidence he had compiled to defend his actions, nothing seemed to be sufficiently convincing. Merely being a member of the Communist Party was enough for the Tartu prison officials and their German overseers to condemn him. When he learned that Asta was dead, his world would have become a grim and lonely place.

As he sat shivering in his cell, Bruno must have questioned how secure his future might have been if he had not joined the Communist Party. While he was the head of the Party's Nominating Committee, he saw what happened to many young Estonian professionals. Those who were lawyers and worked in local government positions, as he had done before the war, were automatically suspected of having nationalist sympathies.

Many were prevented from having any type of meaningful employment. Others were among those Estonians who were deported while many students he knew from the university were conscripted to fight in the Soviet army. None of these paths seemed to offer Bruno any clear options for staying out of harm's way.

Asta was the one person who had given meaning to his life. They had both been committed Estonian patriots. Now she was gone, and he risked being found guilty of being a Communist. Who would know the sacrifice that he had made? Who would even care?

Years later, when my mother finished telling me about her visit with Bruno, she glanced away with a sad sigh. She remembered how disconsolate her sister had been when Bruno was taken to the Tartu prison. She also recalled the fruitless efforts her family had made to defend him. Nothing they had done helped Bruno to prove that he was innocent of the charges against him.

The war, Mom recalled, had upended everyone's life. Two of her uncles were killed by the Soviets. Other people she knew had been executed while many of her neighbors and friends never returned after they were deported to Siberia. Some of the young men Mom knew from school had been conscripted by the Soviets while others were fighting against the Soviets alongside the Finnish army. Millions were dying.

As a young adult, Mom learned that since life could be cruel and capricious, she needed to focus on surviving. In a merciless world where the people you most loved could die, she became determined to stay alive even though her life would always be lonelier without her sister by her side.

CHAPTER 15

THE QUESTION WHY

Having always heard that Bruno was an innocent man who was wrongly arrested, I wondered why the defense material he prepared, coupled with the many support letters in his file, were not sufficient to prove that he had never been a committed member of the Communist Party. In his own defense testimony, he outlined the ways in which he had tried to disrupt and undermine the activities of the Party leaders. Yet, nothing appeared to have swayed the Tartu prison officials.

Within their formal police reports, the Tartu investigators appeared stern, thorough, and skeptical. Staunch anti-Communists, they remained determined throughout their interrogation to root out how Bruno conspired with the Soviet regime, independent of what his initial motivations might have been and separate from his efforts to help the Estonian cause.

Their antipathy was intense, unforgiving, and personal. Many had lost family and friends when the Soviets targeted Estonian military and police officers for arrest, deportation, and execution. The horror of the Soviet efforts to eviscerate

Estonia's military command and police force became clear when the Nazi security police uncovered the mass graves where the Soviets concealed the bodies of the police officers they had killed. In addition, Estonians learned that close to one hundred of the country's top generals and colonels were murdered shortly after they were transported to prison labor camps in Siberia.[62]

Bruno was an anomaly. While the records showed he played a leadership role in the Viljandi Communist Party, there was also evidence that he was working with Estonian resistance groups to subvert the Soviet occupation. Even though the investigators uncovered newspaper articles in which Bruno supported Communism, they also gathered testimony from witnesses who verified Bruno's staunch anti-Communism sentiments.

In mid-March as the Tartu prison officials were wrapping up their investigation, Bruno was led to an interrogation room where several police officers sat waiting with a stenographer. As a brisk wind rattled the windows, Bruno took a seat facing his interrogators for another round of questioning. After spending so much time in his dark cell, the bright sunlight in the room would have made him blink.

The police officers began the meeting by noting the date of the interview. For the record, the stenographer wrote that Investigator Nuri led the questioning of Bruno Kulgma who was an inmate within the Tartu prison. To start the interview, Nuri asked Bruno to explain the extent to which he had been

---

62   Kung, Communism in the Baltic States.

involved in the decisions that were made by the Communist Party leaders in Viljandi.

Nuri's question must have been frustrating for Bruno. He had already answered the same question on multiple other occasions and had also provided written testimony that detailed his limited role within the Communist Party. Recognizing that the Tartu investigators were using a stenographer to create a formal written record of his responses, Bruno reiterated once again that the other members of the Executive Committee were the decision-makers who controlled the policies and activities of the local Communist Party.

"With respect to the structure of the Communist Party in Viljandi County," he testified, "three people were in charge. I was not part of the Party leadership. As Secretary, I attended most of the Executive Committee's meetings since the Party was eager to fill various leadership positions, but my job was limited to presenting those candidates who were seeking membership in the Communist Party and providing background information on them."

To further demonstrate that he had no inside knowledge regarding the Party's deliberations, Bruno explained that his sole purpose for attending the Executive Committee meetings was to assist the Committee members as they decided which of the applicants for Party membership would be accepted. After the deliberations surrounding the nomination process were completed, Bruno asserted that he could gather only a general understanding of the other issues that the Executive Committee planned to discuss once he was gone.

What did Bruno know, Investigator Nuri asked, about the Estonians who were tortured and killed by the Soviet Secret Police? Bruno admitted that he met with an NKVD agent on ten separate occasions when certain Party applicants were accused of being untrustworthy. After he learned which Estonians had come under suspicion, he explained that he sent word to warn them that they were being watched.

"When I heard the Communist Party was investigating certain individuals," he said, "I forwarded this information to those who were at risk. In several cases, I was able to countermand the negative decisions made by the Soviet Secret Police and the Party leaders."

As the head of the Membership Committee, Bruno clarified that he only dealt with complaints regarding those who were seeking membership in Viljandi's Communist Party. The broader investigations that the NKVD instigated against those Estonians suspected of harboring anti-Soviet sentiments were separately conducted apart from the Party apparatus.

"Aside from the situations I have described, the NKVD may have made other complaints to the Party leaders," he said, "but I never heard them myself. There were rumors circulating that the Soviet Secret Police tortured some of those who were arrested, but I had no direct information regarding the complaint process. Nor did I know how the NKVD was responding to the complaints that were made."

Surely, Investigator Nuri pointed out, Bruno must have known about the deportations that the Soviets were planning. What did he imagine was going to happen when hundreds of cattle cars began assembling at the local railway station?

In response, Bruno pointed out that the Party officials were not involved when the Soviet Secret Police and Red Army officers decided who was going to be deported. Nor were the Party members recruited to help arrange for the transports that took place. For his part, Bruno insisted that he had no prior knowledge that the deportations were going to occur.

"I never knew about the deportation planning and did not take part in any of the logistic decisions that were being made. If there were discussions about the upcoming deportations among the Party leaders, I was not invited to those meetings."

Investigator Nuri then asked, "Do you mean to imply that when you were a Party official, you had no dealings with the Red Army?"

Bruno admitted that he was once asked to deliver a letter to the War Commissariat.

"When the Chairman of the Feasibility Committee opened the envelope, he told me that the letter estimated how many horses would be required for the war effort."

Aside from this one meeting, Bruno asserted that he had no other contact with officials in the Soviet military.

Bruno admitted that the War Commissariat tried to recruit volunteers to join the Destruction Battalions after the German army began their advance toward Estonia. When the call for volunteers went out, Bruno testified that he chose instead to join a Home Guard unit in Tänassilma. For the record, he stated that he never took part in any of the crimes committed by the Destruction Battalions.

Investigator Nuri then questioned why Judge Trellin had not been appointed to a position on the Viljandi court. According to Nuri, Trellin had filed a written complaint in which he accused Bruno of being a biased and self-serving opportunist who was only interested in helping his friends from the university.

In response, Bruno explained that as the head of the Membership Committee, he could only recommend candidates for certain positions. The final decisions regarding who was hired for judicial posts were made by a network of committees that the Party had established. As part of their decision-making, one committee reviewed the judges who were already serving on the Viljandi District Court and then decided to retain those who were in place without adding additional judges. That is why, Bruno said, Judge Trellin's application was not considered.

Investigator Nuri then challenged why Bruno had actively promoted Marxist-Leninist theories through his lectures and newspaper articles? If he was an Estonian nationalist as he claimed, why did he write an article for the Viljandi newspaper that encouraged the town residents to visit a reading room filled with Communist propaganda? Bruno pointed out that the reading room contained only Russian-language material that the Party received from Moscow.

He may have been forced to act as a Party spokesman, but Bruno stated that he never participated in any of the Communist plans to subvert Estonian society. He emphasized that he did not approve of, nor did he advocate for, the collectivization of privately-owned land. As proof of his intentions, he disavowed his Communist Party affiliation as soon as he was able once the German invasion had begun.

"It was my intention to escape the Communists," he said. "In fact, I did so on July 3, 1941, after one of my colleagues from the university was arrested."

In conclusion, Bruno reminded the Tartu investigators that he had already provided a written statement in which he detailed the decision-making hierarchy within the Viljandi Communist Party. In the same document, he emphasized his own limited scope of responsibilities. As part of his testimony, he also pointed out that he had supplied a lengthy list of potential witnesses who could confirm that his account regarding his actions and motivations was truthful.

"I have nothing further to explain," he said. "I have tried to correct any errors and falsehoods in the testimony against me. Beyond that, I have nothing further to add."

After interrogating Bruno, the Tartu investigators interviewed five additional witnesses. When they questioned Karl Leetma, a judge from the Viljandi District Court, Leetma confirmed that Bruno was a member of the Estonian Students' Society fraternity at the University of Tartu and was also part of a group that plotted to sabotage the Soviet occupation.

Having known Bruno for many years, Leetma testified that he was not, nor had he ever been, a Communist. Along with other Estonian partisans, Bruno's sole purpose, Leetma contended, was to protect the cause of Estonian nationalism until the country could once again be independent.

To corroborate Leetma's testimony, the investigators interviewed Elmar Jaaste, an accountant from Viljandi. Jaaste confirmed that Bruno decided to join the Party to undermine the Communists when they threatened to take control of Estonia's government and businesses. Jasste's statements were corroborated by a third witness, Ernst Rusi, who was an elementary school teacher from Tänassilma. Rusi affirmed that Bruno was not a Communist. Instead, he characterized Bruno as a patriot who fought alongside the Home Guard partisans when they defended the town from the Soviet Destruction Battalions.

As part of their efforts to gather more evidence, the Tartu investigators questioned Harry Neumann, a Viljandi banker. During one of his earlier interrogations, Bruno alleged that

Neumann once worked for the Soviet Secret Police and in that capacity submitted a complaint letter to the Party in which he accused two other bank officials of having anti-Soviet sentiments. Rather than share the letter with Party leaders, Bruno told the Tartu investigators that he destroyed the incriminating accusations.

When asked about Bruno's charges, Neumann denied that he ever collaborated with the Soviet Secret Police. He stated that he was unsure why Bruno had fabricated these allegations, particularly since the Estonian investigators had no evidence that implicated him as a Soviet agent.

As their final witness the Tartu police questioned Endel Roots. According to Bruno, Roots was a trade school graduate who joined the Communist Party at the age of nineteen. Initially, the Party appointed Roots to be a school inspector, but Bruno indicated that he was later fired. When interviewed by the Tartu police, Roots charged that Bruno was only defaming Roots' reputation to deflect attention from himself.

According to Roots, the leaders of the Communist Party in Viljandi were old men who had trouble making decisions. Bruno, Roots claimed, was the one who was really pulling the strings. As head of the Membership Committee, it was Bruno who controlled who could join the Party and who received important jobs. Roots further asserted that Bruno reveled in his power over others and only promoted those he liked while firing anyone who challenged him.

After completing their final witness interviews at the beginning of April, the Tartu investigators compiled their findings against Bruno in a summary case report. The voluminous evidence they had collected was then placed in a thick binder that included Bruno's written testimony, the several dozen support letters filed on his behalf, the transcripts from his interrogations, and the summary notes from the witness interviews. The investigators then summarized their findings on a single sheet of paper.

At the start, the investigators identified Bruno Kulgma as a single man who resided in Viljandi. They noted that Bruno was a law school graduate who had been employed as the Assistant Municipal Secretary for the town of Tänassilma. Prior to his arrest, Bruno had no previous criminal record nor was there any evidence that he had been politically active before joining the Communist Party. After being taken into custody on October 14, 1941, Bruno was identified as a prisoner within the Tartu prison.

After the police completed their summary report in Estonian, it was translated into German. While the two versions were nearly identical, several damning modifications were added to the German language text.

Both reports detailed how Bruno met with several Party officials after the Communists came to power in Estonia and then applied to become a member of the Communist Party on July 29, 1940. In the Estonian version of the report, the investigators stated that after being offered several leadership positions, Bruno chose to become the head of the Membership Committee on August 29. Within the German translation, Bruno was further identified as occupying the position of second Secretary in the Party's leadership cadre.

The Tartu investigators explained how Bruno, as head of the Membership Committee, was able to place Estonian officials in key jobs by vouching for their political allegiances. They cited testimony by the Mayor of Viljandi who asserted that Bruno used his position within the Communist Party to defend the interests of Estonian nationals.

The German translation added that Bruno met with the NKVD on ten separate occasions to discuss the placement of officials in key posts. The text exaggerated Bruno's authority and failed to mention that Bruno protected his fellow Estonians by alerting them when they were under surveillance by the NKVD.

In both versions of the indictment, Bruno was accused of selectively awarding jobs to colleagues from his student fraternity. Neither of the accounts identified these associates as part of a resistance network of Estonian nationals who were working to undermine the Soviet occupation.

Without any supporting evidence, the German text also charged that Bruno favored the job applications submitted by Jewish attorneys over those filed by nationalist-minded businessmen, retailers, industrialists, and political officials or their family members. The accusation must have been added to satisfy the German authorities since the Tartu investigators had not collected any evidence that this accusation was true.

In January 1941, the investigators pointed out that after Bruno was released from his position as head of the Membership Committee, he was elevated to the position of Chairman of the Viljandi County Party. While occupying this role, he gave thirteen lectures and wrote four newspaper articles regarding Communist Party doctrines. In addition to promoting Party activities, he also compiled Communist propaganda material which he placed in a library reading room. The investigators failed to acknowledge that when these events occurred, Bruno was under surveillance by the NKVD. Nor did they include Bruno's assertions that as Chairman, he became a Party spokesman, but had no decision-making authority.

To aid the Soviet war effort, Bruno was reported to have helped requisition horses for the Red Army. The assertion was a clear exaggeration of Bruno's testimony that he merely delivered a letter in which Soviet military officials estimated the number of horses that might be required for future war efforts.

On July 2, 1941, the Tartu investigators noted that Bruno joined a Home Guard partisan unit to protect Tänassilma from attacks by the Soviet sponsored Destruction Battalions. Bruno was also credited with helping police investigators to identify other defendants who were Communist Party members and NKVD agents.

In summary, the report concluded that Bruno was an active member of the Communist Party who publicly promoted Marxist ideology. While the investigators acknowledged that Bruno had indeed worked to help his fellow Estonians, they alleged he showed partiality and favoritism when he decided those who he was going to help.

Within Bruno's folder, there was no indication that Bruno was given an opportunity to refute the conclusions that the Tartu investigators had reached. Nor was there any reference to the more than fifty witnesses who were willing to testify that Bruno was not, nor had he ever been a loyal member of the Communist Party.

Once the case report was approved by the German prison authorities, the three-man tribunal met to review the findings and to determine Bruno's fate. They did not create a formal set of minutes from their meeting. The names of the tribunal members who reviewed Bruno's case report were not listed.

Nor did they indicate the date when they met or what factors were taken into consideration when Bruno was sentenced. The tribunal's final decision was summarized on a single sheet of paper. Bruno, the tribunal concluded, was guilty.

Based on the findings from the Tartu police investigators, the tribunal recommended that Bruno should be imprisoned in a labor camp for the duration of the war. They also specified that this sentence was subject to review by the German high command. After Commandant Fahrnberger, the Nazi official who supervised the Tartu prison, received the sentencing recommendation, he countermanded the tribunal's decision and ordered Bruno to be executed by a firing squad. There was no opportunity for Bruno to appeal the decision.

Within the German sentencing ledger, Bruno was listed as having been found guilty of being a member of the Estonian Communist Party. In addition to being the Party Secretary, he was also identified as the Head of the Communist Party for Viljandi County. By order of the German Security Police, Bruno Kulgma was sentenced to be executed on April 22, 1942.

Even though the Estonian police, both in Viljandi and in Tartu, had compiled evidence from more than a dozen witnesses during their ten-month investigation that confirmed Bruno's Estonian loyalties, the tribunal charged that Bruno was an active member of the Communist Party. Following Martin Sandberger's order that all Communists should receive the harshest possible sentence, no countervailing evidence was considered, nor did the sentencing recommendation from the Estonian tribunal deter the German prison commandant from condemning Bruno to death.

When Commandant Fahnrberger imposed Bruno's death sentence, he did not justify his decision based on any evidence that Bruno represented a dangerous security risk to Germany's armed forces. The fact that Bruno had fought alongside a band of Estonian partisans against the Soviet Destruction Battalions and the evacuating Red Army was not taken into consideration. From the perspective of the Germans who controlled Estonia's jails and prisons all that mattered was that Bruno was a Communist who deserved to die.

Bruno's Communist Party identification card

After spending more than five months at the Tartu prison, Bruno must have realized that it would only be a matter of time before he would learn his fate. He knew that the Germans were dictating who would live and who would die. He also knew that he would have no opportunity to defend himself or to appeal the sentence against him.

When Bruno was told that he was being transferred to the Death Barracks on the evening of April 21, he would not have been surprised. Over the past months, he had watched as other fellow prisoners were condemned to death for being Communists based on even less robust evidence than Bruno knew that his own file contained.

During the previous year, while he worked to undermine the Communist Party, Bruno recognized how easily he could have been sentenced to death by the Soviet Secret Police. He knew that the Soviets were executing any Estonians who resisted the Soviet occupation. Others were deported solely for being Estonian nationalists.

While the Soviets labelled those Estonians who fought against the Soviet occupation as traitors, the Germans accused Estonians of treason if they had any connection with the Soviets or the Communist Party. Estonians who supported the Germans were called Fascists while those who aligned with the Soviets were Communists. There was no middle ground to be an Estonian patriot.

At twenty-seven, Bruno would have expected that his whole life would still be in front of him. As he remembered the years that he devoted to working his way through law school, he recalled how he hoped to become a lawyer who defended Estonian laws. Instead, he found himself trying to resist the legal systems that were imposed on Estonia by the Soviets and the Germans, both of which defined Estonian nationalism as an act of defiance and treason.

As he pondered how it was that he found himself facing a firing squad, Bruno would have wondered whether any additional evidence could have changed the verdict that the Estonian investigators reached. He would also have questioned why the punishment he was facing was out of proportion with the crimes he was alleged to have committed.

As a low-level functionary within the Communist Party who had no decision-making authority, he could not have imagined that he would be held responsible for the terror the Soviets caused during their occupation. Yet, to his misfortune he became one of the few Party officials who remained in Estonia to take the blame.

The hours would have passed slowly on Bruno's last night. At some point, he was visited by the Estonian guard who had helped him in the past. He was the one who passed Bruno's message to Asta. He also helped arrange my mother's visit when she came to the Tartu prison to let Bruno know that Asta had died.

The two men likely sat together in silence, as they pondered the injustice of Bruno's upcoming execution. Knowing how close Bruno was to the Vares family, the guard promised that he would inform them that Bruno had died. Based on his experience with the firing squads, he would have also reassured Bruno that his death would be quick and painless. What else was there to say?

CHAPTER 16

BRUNO'S EXECUTION

April was the month when Estonian farmers typically released their cattle into the fields, freeing them to graze in the greening pastures after a long winter confinement. April was also the start of the growing season when gardeners like Bruno's mother would begin preparing their spring beds, tenderly digging up the soil, and then covering their newly planted seeds with dirt.

However dismayed, frustrated, and angry Bruno must have been when he learned that he was being transferred to the Death Barracks, he was probably glad that his deceased mother would not have to learn that her son was killed by a firing squad. He would also have been relieved that Asta who spent years worrying about him would be spared the pain of finding out that he had been executed.

As World War II raged on, Bruno knew many close friends and colleagues who were losing their lives on the battlefield. It was a sacrifice they agreed to accept when they chose to fight in defense of the patriotic values they espoused. With his own death drawing near, Bruno likely tried to keep in mind the commitment he himself had made to defend his country and his countrymen.

He had fought like a soldier on a battlefield in a war that was still very much under way. All that he could hope for was that whenever the fighting finally came to an end, his beloved Estonia would once again regain its independence, however long that might take.

As the sun came up the next morning, the weather was windy and cold. While the guards who volunteered to serve as the execution squad gathered in the prison courtyard, a driver parked a bus near the entrance to the prison. The Estonian official in charge of the execution team then stepped forward carrying a clipboard with the names of the dozen prisoners who were slated to be killed.

As he shouted out each name, the doomed prisoners were escorted from their cells and then lined up in a row where they shivered in the brisk April wind. Soon after Bruno joined the group, the inmates were ordered to take off their shoes and remove all their clothes down to their underwear.

With his fingers stiffening in the frigid morning air, Bruno would have struggled to loosen his shoelaces and undo his shirt buttons. After removing his pants, he left his clothes in a pile and then followed his fellow prisoners to the nearby bus. Before the prisoners were allowed to board, the Estonian guards bound their hands behind their backs and then joined the prisoners together with a single rope.

Hobbling in an awkward row, the condemned inmates then climbed onto the bus and stood in silence as the Estonian guards who would be their executioners climbed on board. As the bus pulled away from the prison, a bitter smell of fear and urine began wafting through the air. The journey to the Jakala Trench on the outskirts of Tartu did not take long.

The sky was overcast and cloudy as the bus parked at its designated stop. After the prisoners were ordered to walk toward the awaiting trench, they struggled to keep their balance as their bare feet slipped on the frozen ground. Still tied together, they made their way along a well-trodden path through some fields, as they numbly approached the space ahead where the Estonian guards were already lining up.

In the distance, they could hear the sharp cawing of crows that nested in the nearby trees. While some Estonians considered the black birds to be harbingers of death, Bruno would likely have remembered that Asta's family name, Vares, meant "crow" in the Estonian language. Perhaps Asta's spirit was nearby. Perhaps he would soon be by her side.

After the inmates reached the edge of the trench, they were ordered as a group to kneel while the Estonian guards lined up one by one behind them. Quietly weeping, they struggled to remain upright as loose gravel bit into their knees. In front of them, a sharp smell of lime wafted from the open pit that barely covered the stench of decaying flesh. It was the smell of death.

Once the prisoners were in position, the Commandant of the Guards announced their verdicts. Turning toward the prisoners, he declared, "In the name of the Republic of Estonia, you have been found guilty of crimes against the Fatherland and are sentenced to death."[63] Bruno probably found it ironic

---

63   U.S. District Court for the Eastern Region of New York, "U.S. v Karl Linnas."

that he was about to be executed for committing crimes against Estonia.

As the contingent of Estonian guards positioned themselves behind each of the prisoners, they readied their weapons.[64] Rather than look at the entangled arms and legs in the pit below him, Bruno must have glanced towards the clouds racing across the sky. After the prison commander gave the order to fire, the last sound Bruno heard was the sharp crack of the bullets as they exploded from the rifles that the guards had aimed at each prisoner's head. Is this how Bruno could ever have imagined that his life would end?

Sixty years after Bruno was killed, my mother was still angry when she remembered the injustice of his death. During one of my many visits with her, we sat on the patio outside her home on a May afternoon. A light springtime breeze rustled in the nearby trees where the leaves were turning a pale shade of green.

Still puzzling over what happened to Bruno, I asked Mom how she had found out that he had died. She sighed and glanced away with a pained look in her eyes, as she recalled the fruitless efforts her family had made to save him.

"We spent weeks contacting everyone we knew, looking for anyone who could speak on Bruno's behalf. But once he was moved to Tartu, we no longer had any influence. It was so hard to get any news. No one could tell us when he was going to trial and how we might be able to defend him."

After she visited Bruno to tell him that Asta had died, my mother remained convinced that Bruno would ultimately

---

64   Weiss-Wendt, On the Margins.

be found innocent. Like most people in Tartu, she had heard rumors about the executions that were taking place on the outskirts of town, but she never imagined that Bruno would be killed.

When her spring semester at the University of Tartu ended, Mom returned to Viljandi where she was hired to work as a laboratory assistant at a nearby medical clinic. She was twenty-one, still unsure whether she wanted to study medicine, but nonetheless excited about the job she was about to start. Since my grandmother had moved Jaan, my mother's younger brother, into the bedroom that she once shared with Asta, Mom was arranging to move into a small apartment in town with her friend, Helga.

On a Saturday morning as she was packing her clothes, she was surprised to hear the front doorbell ring. Her father's clinic was closed for the weekend and most neighbors who came to visit entered the family apartment through the back screened-in porch.

When she went to see who rang the bell, she was startled to see her young neighbor who worked at the Tartu prison. He stood awkwardly on the front stoop with his eyes lowered and his head hung low. Before she had time to say anything, he handed over a package.

Mom was confused when she took the bundle. It was heavy and awkwardly covered with loose paper wrapping. Then she noticed a pair of shoes and a man's grey suit jacket. Looking more closely, she gasped when she recognized the guard was giving her Bruno's clothes.

Not wanting to accept the cold reality that Bruno could be gone, she asked,

"Does this mean Bruno is dead?"

The guard simply nodded his head and turned to leave.

Only three months earlier, Mom had lost her sister. Now Asta's fiancée was also dead. Given the intense fighting between the Germans and the Soviets, death was all around her. But the loss of Bruno, so soon after Asta died, was devastating.

When she first heard the news, Mom was unwilling to believe that Bruno could have been executed. She did not ask the guard how or when he was killed. Nor did she want to know where he had died. The painful news that he was gone was all she could bear.

Only a year earlier, Bruno was living on the second floor of the family's home and making plans with Asta for their life together. They were two young people of promise who had hoped to share a future together. No one could explain how both could be dead. All my mother knew and cared about was the stark fact that they were not coming back.

Mom did not share any details about the guard who delivered Bruno's clothes. Like other young Estonian men, he found a job working at the Tartu prison, a position that was preferrable to fighting on the front lines. As a lowly private, he would have been required to follow the orders from the prison commanders without questioning what was right or wrong. Yet, he was still willing to do one last favor for Bruno by letting the Vares family know that Bruno had been killed.

Aside from my mother's family and the Tartu prison guard, few residents of Viljandi were aware that Bruno had been executed. The only notice of his death was recorded in the ledger where the Germans enumerated the enemies of the Third Reich who were executed. To justify his death sentence, the sparse entry in the German ledger condemned Bruno for collaborating with the Communists. No other public obituaries marked Bruno's passing.

If Bruno had been able to survive once World War II ended, he risked being convicted by the Soviets as a traitor to the Communist cause, given the extensive records that documented how he worked to sabotage the first Soviet occupation. Who knows what kind of life he could have lived, if instead of remaining in Estonia, Bruno had joined my mother's family when they escaped?

Mom always blamed the Soviets for Bruno's death, arguing that, if the Soviet Union had not invaded Estonia, Bruno would never have lost his life. In this alternative version of what could have happened, she hoped that Asta, too, would have been able to survive.

My mother died before I could tell her what I later learned from Bruno's prison files. If she could have read through the defense material that Bruno compiled, I believe she would have been proud at how he defended his actions. She would have applauded the precise way in which he documented all the ways he tried to fight against the Soviet plans to take over Estonia's government, businesses, schools, courts and hospitals. Among the materials that supported Bruno's innocence, she would have also been heartened to see how many Estonians spoke on Bruno's behalf even if, in the end, their support did not help to save his life.

Yet, even knowing more about how Bruno tried to defend himself, I believe my mother would still have remained bitter that he was never recognized for his heroic sacrifice. After Estonia was occupied by the Soviets and the Germans, being an Estonian patriot had no meaning. For my mother, Bruno's story was part of a larger narrative that was rarely discussed, and that few of her acquaintances understood.

CHAPTER 17

POSTWAR SYSTEMS OF JUSTICE

Within the Soviet Union, World War II continues to be remembered as the Great Patriotic War in which the heroic Soviet military defeated the forces of Nazi Germany. Among all the Allied countries, the Soviet Union suffered the greatest number of casualties with twenty-six million killed.[65] Soviet forces also assumed a major role in forcing Adolf Hitler's army to retreat from the Eastern Front.

Yet, at the end of World War II, little attention was given to the 1939 agreement in which Joseph Stalin and Adolf Hitler divided up Polish territory and placed the Baltic states within the Soviet sphere of influence. While many in the Western world chose to overlook the Soviet invasion of Poland, those in Eastern Europe who suffered under the brutal Soviet occupation have a different perspective on the Soviet's role during World War II.

---

65   Ellman and Maksudov, "Soviet Deaths."

When officials from the U.S. State Department released the full details of the Molotov-Von Ribbentrop Pact in 1948, Joseph Stalin denied that he ever conspired with Hitler to carve up Polish territory. In his 1948 book, *Falsifiers of History*, the Soviet leader claimed the allegation that his country entered into an agreement with Adolf Hitler was totally false. In his words,

"It would be gross slander to assert that the conclusion of the Pact with the Hitlerites was part of the U.S.S.R.'s foreign policy."[66]

Although the State Department released information regarding the Pact's secret addendum that emboldened the Soviets to occupy the Baltic states, Stalin asserted that the three Baltic countries voluntarily petitioned to become part of the U.S.S.R. The Soviets, Stalin asserted, had merely responded to the wishes of the citizens of Estonia, Latvia, and Lithuania when they expressed a desire to join the Soviet Union. In Stalin's view,

"Only enemies of democracy or people who had lost their senses could describe those actions of the Soviet government as aggression."[67]

After Germany was defeated, jurists from the Soviet Union took a lead role in establishing the legal framework under which the war crimes committed by Nazi Germany would be prosecuted. As part of the pretrial protocols, Soviet lawyers identified the topics they insisted should not be brought up during the trials. The list included details regarding

---

66   "Falsifiers of History," Wikipedia.

67   "Falsifiers of History," Wikipedia.

the Molotov-Ribbentrop Pact, references to the visits German Foreign Minister Ribbentrop made to Moscow, and questions regarding the "Soviet Baltic republics."[68]

Despite the efforts made by the Soviet legal team to limit testimony in the Nuremberg courtroom, Joachim von Ribbentrop, Germany's Minister of Foreign Affairs, openly asserted during his trial that the Soviets, along with Germany, were equally complicit in the occupation of Poland.

As part of Ribbentrop's defense, his attorney, Dr. Martin Horn questioned how Ribbentrop could be condemned by the Soviets when the Soviet Union had ratified a well-publicized Pact with Nazi Germany and had later invaded Polish territory. Calling Horn's statements irrelevant and provocative, the Soviet prosecutors refused to allow any further evidence regarding the Molotov-Ribbentrop Pact to be introduced during the trial of the German foreign minister.[69]

Undeterred, Ribbentrop continued to insist that the Soviets were also guilty of war crimes. In his final statement, he condemned Stalin for wanting to take over the Baltic states.

"When I went to see Marshal Stalin at Moscow in 1939, he did not discuss with me the peaceful settlement of the German-Polish conflict," Ribbentrop testified, "But rather he hinted that if, in addition to half of Poland and the Baltic countries, he did not receive Lithuania and the harbor of Libau, I might as well return home."[70]

---

68   Hirsh, "The Soviets at Nuremberg."

69   UPI Archives, "Profiles of the 21 Nazi Leaders."

70   Bush, "An Investigation into the Trial of a Nazi War Criminal."

Ribbentrop's continued efforts to introduce evidence regarding the complicity of the Soviets would be unsuccessful. While he was being sentenced to death for war crimes in the fall of 1946, his Soviet counterpart, Vyacheslav Molotov, was meeting with representatives from Great Britain and the United States to craft a series of postwar agreements.

Two weeks after his conviction, Ribbentrop became the first Nazi official to face the gallows. At eleven minutes past 1:00 on October 16, 1946, the white-faced German foreign minister walked thirteen steps to a platform where he weakly stated his name. After a black hood was placed over his head, the guards wrapped a noose around his neck and bound his feet with a webbed Army belt. When the assistant executor pulled the lever, Ribbentrop's body disappeared while the gallows rope tightened around his neck. For the next fourteen minutes, he swung from side to side until he finally choked to death. After he was declared dead, his ashes were scattered in the Isar River.[71]

Remembering Ribbentrop's war crimes trial, Mom said,

"No one had any sympathy for Ribbentrop or the other Nazi generals who helped Hitler wage his war. We were just waiting for the Soviet war crimes to be investigated, but that never happened."

For the next several decades, diplomats from the Soviet Union blocked any discussion at the United Nations regarding Baltic independence despite the annual demonstrations mounted by Baltic activists on the anniversary of the day when the Molotov-Ribbentrop Pact was signed. While the

---

71   Zeller, 'The Nuremberg Hangings."

protestors continued to question the legality of his namesake agreement, Molotov was living a quiet life as a retiree in a Moscow suburb. Even though Stalin deported Molotov's wife on charges that she was a Zionist spy, Molotov remained a strong supporter of Stalin's policies. After retiring from public life, he spent his days at the Lenin Library gathering materials for his memoir.

Shortly before he died, Molotov was asked by an interviewer whether he believed Stalin was deceived by Hitler when the Germans reneged on the 1939 Pact. Dismissing the idea, the former Soviet foreign minister scoffed, "Stalin trusted Hitler? He didn't trust his own people."

Reflecting on the Stalinist purges and deportations, Molotov admitted the repressive policies were severe, but he claimed they were necessary.

"I never regretted and will never regret that we acted very harshly," Molotov said. "But mistakes did occur."[72]

Compared with Ribbentrop's ignominious end, Molotov was buried in a place of honor at Novodevichy Cemetery when he died at the age of ninety-six in 1986. Throughout his long career, he would never be admonished for his role in negotiating the agreement that not only partitioned Poland, but also kept the Baltic states under Soviet control for the duration of his life. Nor did any international courts of law address Molotov's involvement in the illegal deportation of tens of thousands of Baltic residents who were transported to Siberia where many died.

---

72   Roberts, Molotov: Stalin's Cold Warrior, 14.

Molotov was not the only World War II figure who managed to escape justice. Even though Martin Sandberger had ordered thousands of Estonian Jews and Communists to be executed, he was able to return to civilian life after spending only a decade in prison. Despite the extensive crimes against humanity that occurred in Estonia under his command, Sandberger continued to assert for the duration of his life that he was innocent.

During his trial at Nuremberg, Sandberger contended that he was only following the orders he received from his superior officer when he commanded his troops to execute Jews, Communists, and others considered to be enemies of the Third Reich.[73] Moreover, he noted that during the war, he himself never killed anyone. Instead, the Estonian guards were the ones who were guilty of carrying out the executions.

In Sandberger's defense, his attorney, Dr. Stein, argued that Sandberger was reacting to the danger posed by partisans who threatened the lines of communication to the German Army Group North during its assault on Leningrad.

"The measures against Communist activists were harsh," Stein argued, "But considering the general situation of the war and the special position of Estonia, they were justified, and the defendant was convinced of it."

The Nuremberg prosecutors refuted Sandberger's claim that the Jews were partisans. They also countered Sandberger's assertion that prisoners were given access to due process protections or any other legal remedies. As demonstrated in Bruno's prison files, the tribunal at the Tartu prison operated

---

73   "Martin Sandberger," Wikipedia.

without any type of trial proceedings during which defendants could present evidence in their own defense or appeal the sentences they received.

At the conclusion of Sandberger's trial, the Nuremberg judges determined that the Nazi Commandant had willingly obeyed his German superiors. They also found that the Estonian militia was under Sandberger's control when thousands of Estonian civilians were sentenced to death. After finding Sandberger responsible for crimes against humanity, the court sentenced him to death by hanging.[74]

America's lead prosecutor, Benjamin Ferencz concurred with Sandberger's sentence, writing, "Sandberger was an active and presumably even a zealous member of the band of murderers who killed hundreds of thousands of innocent people. His death sentence was well deserved."

After Sandberger's conviction, his attorneys continued to appeal the judgement against him, claiming that their client was a man of good character who did not agree with Hitler's orders. In defense of his son, Sandberger's father portrayed Martin as a naïve idealist who was duped into supporting the National Socialists while he was a student.[75]

Other petitioners described Sandberger as a loving husband and father, a Christian who rejected hatred, and someone who had never been hostile to Jews. Among the lengthy appeals filed on Sandberger's behalf, Bishop Wurm

---

74 Traces of War, "Martin Sandberger."

75 Earl, "Good Nazis and Other Germans," 73.

claimed the uncertainty Sandberger faced regarding his fate was inhumane and contrary to all feelings of decency.[76]

Three years after Sandberger's conviction, in 1951 John McCloy, the U.S. High Commissioner for Germany, responded to pressure from Sandberger's defenders, and commuted Sandberger's death sentence to life imprisonment. Despite the reprieve, the appeals filed on Sandberger's behalf continued for the next ten years.

In their filings, Sandberger's lawyers described the Nazi Commandant as having been "cleansed" by his prison experience. The young attorney, they argued, was just starting his life and deserved an opportunity to prove himself anew. Sandberger's wartime exhortations in which he urged his German soldiers to set aside all considerations of decency and humanity were not mentioned.

In 1958, Sandberger's attorneys were finally successful in having their client's sentence commuted. After spending nearly ten years in prison, Martin Sandberger won his release and began a career as a corporate lawyer.

Although a German prosecutor in Stuttgart tried in 1970 to reopen an investigation into Sandberger's wartime activities, the court determined that the former Nazi could not be resentenced for crimes for which he had already been prosecuted.

During a postwar interview, Sandberger was asked by an interviewer whether he believed that he deserved the death penalty that came down from the Nuremberg court. In response, Sandberger complained that the Allied legal

---

76   Earl, "Good Nazis and Other Germans," 79.

teams had imposed their own standard of justice while they prosecuted the case against him, a process that Sandberger contended was illegal.

It was unfair, he claimed, for German defendants to be charged with war crimes based on legal standards defined by the Allied victors many years after the alleged events had occurred. He neglected to point out that Germany had imposed its own system of law on Estonia with even more calamitous consequences.

Sandberger further contended that the members of the German Secret Police were honorable men who followed the strictest legal standards.

"It was not policy, or okay within the [German Secret Police]," Sandberger argued, "to shoot prisoners or civilians unless a trial [occurred] and lawful orders came from the top."[77]

While Sandberger insisted that all proper legal procedures were followed under his command, the prisoners he condemned in Estonia did not receive any type of trial. Nor did they benefit from the appeals process that protected Sandberger from being executed.

Nearly fifty years after Sandberger had been released from prison, a journalist from *Der Spiegel* found the 98-year-old former Nazi living in a Christian retirement home. When he was interviewed in 2010, a month before he died, the ailing Sandberger sat stiffly in an armchair while he was asked what he remembered from the war years.

---

77   Mourning the Ancients, "Dr. Martin Sandberger,"

Surrounded by a bound collection of Swabian folk tales, black-and-white photos of his deceased relatives, and an old television set, the former German Commandant appeared at first to have fallen asleep and then replied in a squeaky voice,

"What I remember is completely irrelevant."

During his 2010 interview, Sandberger willingly described his life in Berlin before the war as well as his years in the German Waffen-SS. When asked about the Nazi policies that promoted racial genocide, he claimed, "I wasn't heavily involved in all that."[78]

His memory of the detailed progress reports where he bragged about his success in exterminating Jews and Communists appeared to have faded away. He could not remember supervising the deportation of Jews and Polish citizens from Poland. Nor did he recall arranging for the transport of Jews from Strasbourg, France. His exhortations that Communists deserved to be killed were forgotten along with the carefully written notations in which he judged which prisoners deserved death by hanging.

When he was asked in 2010 whether he felt ashamed for the thousands who were killed at his command, Sandberger was silent for a long time before saying, "I don't want to talk about it." He died a few months later at the age of 98, unrepentant and unforgiving.[79] To the end, Sandberger remained convinced that the Estonians who were executed under his orders deserved to die.

---

78   Mayr, "The Quiet Death of a Nazi."

79   "Martin Sandberger," Wikipedia.

CHAPTER 18

WHICH SIDE TO JOIN

Given the role Vyacheslav Molotov played in facilitating the first Soviet invasion of Estonia in 1939 as well as his part in justifying the more permanent occupation that occurred after the war, I questioned why neither he nor any other Soviet leaders were held accountable for the crimes that were committed while the Soviets occupied Estonia.

When Estonia regained its independence in 1991, nearly fifty years after World War II ended, Lennart Meri, Estonia's first president, recognized the importance of acknowledging and coming to terms with the country's wartime experiences. Estonia, he wrote, should seek to document its historical past not for revenge but for the purpose of understanding.

In his words, "A winner is recognized by forgiveness."[80]

Meri's own personal history mirrored the complex ways in which Estonian families struggled to navigate the successive occupations of their country by the Soviet Union

---

80   Estonian State Commission, "The White Book," 69.

and Germany. As the son of an Estonian diplomat, he learned to speak five languages fluently. After the Soviets arrested his family and deported them to Siberia in 1940, twelve-year-old Lennart supported his parents by working as a lumberman and potato peeler.

Six years later, when the family was able to return to Estonia, Lennart attended the University of Tartu. While Estonia was occupied by the Soviet Union, he was unable to work as a historian, and instead became involved with a well-established theater in Tartu while producing radio plays. Through his writing and speeches, Meri continued to promote Estonian independence and in 1990 was chosen to become the country's Minister of Foreign Affairs. He was later elected to be the president of Estonia in 1992.[81]

By contrast, Lennart's cousin, Arnold Meri, was a life-long supporter of the Soviet occupation of Estonia. When he was a young boy, Arnold's family emigrated to Yugoslavia where he was educated in Russian schools. During the first Soviet occupation of Estonia in 1940, Arnold joined the Red Army where he served as a deputy political officer. Wounded several times in battles against the German army, he became the first Estonian to be awarded a medal for bravery by the Soviets when he received the Order of Lenin, the highest honor in the U.S.S.R. in 1948.

Reflecting on his choice to collaborate with the Soviets, Arnold said,

---

81   "Lennart Meri," Wikipedia.

"Every Estonian had only one decision to make, whose side to take in that bloody fight— the Nazis' or the anti-Hitler coalition's."[82]

After returning to Soviet-occupied Estonia at the end of the war, Arnold became a member of the Central Committee of the Communist Party of Estonia and worked with the Leninist Young Communist League. Estonian prosecutors would later accuse Arnold of helping to deport 251 Estonians from the island of Hiiumaa in 1949.

When he was put on trial in 2007, Arnold contended that he was only responsible for monitoring whether current laws were being followed during the deportation process. He also stated that he tried to protect the deportees by ensuring they could travel with their full allotment of personal possessions.

After he recognized that abuses were occurring, Arnold withdrew from his government position in 1951. In response, the Communist Party expelled him and stripped him of his military awards. After being rehabilitated by Soviet authorities five years later, he was appointed to be a member of the U.S.S.R. Supreme Council.

When, decades later, Estonian prosecutors charged him with crimes against humanity, Arnold's lawyer, Sven Sillar, argued that rather than being a KGB accomplice, Arnold Meri acted as an ombudsman who defended people's rights.[83]

In further support of Meri's innocence, the Russian Duma called on the European Parliament to stop the "shameful" proceedings, stating,

---

82 "Arnold Meri." Wikipedia.

83 Chivers, "Cousin Charged with Genocide."

"(Meri's) trial is a purely political attempt to revise the results of WWII and to discredit the efforts of the anti-Hitler coalition to save mankind from the Fascist plague."[84]

Since Arnold was deaf, nearly blind, and suffered from high blood pressure, his family hoped he would be declared unfit to stand trial. In the end, he died in his sleep at the age of 89 before his trial could be completed. Hours after his death, Russian President Dmitry Medvedev awarded Arnold Meri a posthumous Medal of Honor.

As they sought to document Soviet war crimes, the Estonian prosecutors investigated several hundred potential cases, but only brought charges against twenty-four defendants. Their efforts were hampered by the lack of evidence, much of which had either been destroyed, lost or was no longer unavailable. The more prominent Soviet leaders who orchestrated the deportations were either dead or living in obscurity in Russia while many of those who could be tried were elderly and frail. In several prominent cases, the prosecutors were forced to suspend the trial proceedings when the defendants either became seriously ill or died.

As part of their prosecutions, the Estonian lawyers did not seek harsh punishments. Instead, they hoped to use the proceedings as public forums where information that had formerly been suppressed by the Soviets could finally be revealed.[85] The public court proceedings also enabled those who had been victimized by the deportations to confront

---

84   "Arnold Meri," Wikipedia.

85   Liivoja, "Soviet War Crimes in the Baltic States.".

the perpetrators who arranged for them to be transported to Siberia.

Idel Jakobson was among the first to be charged by the Estonian prosecutors for committing crimes against humanity during the Soviet occupation in 1940. As part of their investigation, the attorneys compiled thirty-two volumes of documentary evidence that implicated Jakobson in the murder of the Estonian police who were executed at the Pirita-Kosel site—the place where my grandfather's brother, Jakob, was killed.

Jakobson was accused of arranging for eighteen hundred Estonians to be tortured and of sentencing twelve hundred people to death without the benefit of a trial.[86] He was also charged with executing 622 people at the Sosva Vostok-Uraliski Prison Camp in Siberia.[87] Despite the efforts of the prosecutors to convict Jakobson, the 93-year-old defendant became ill and died before his trial could be concluded.[88]

While they were being prosecuted, the Soviet guards who were indicted for helping to deport Estonian citizens argued that they were merely following orders, a defense that was often used during the Nuremberg trials. One guard, 77-year-old Johannes Klaassepp testified,

"When my boss ordered me to produce an official document on the family status of a person, I did. I don't think it's a terrible crime against humanity."[89]

---

86   Kaitsepolitseiamet, "Judicial Decisions."

87   "Idel Jakobson," Wikipedia.

88   Kaitsepolitseiamet, "Judicial Decisions.".

89   Berendson, "The Deportee Rejects the Charges,"

For his part, Jüri Karpov contended that when he signed deportation orders, he only arrested illegal immigrants or those who were suspected of espionage. As he sat in in the court room wearing thick bifocals, the 81-year-old Karpov explained,

"My duty was to learn the addresses my superiors were looking for... I did not speak, nor do I now speak Estonian and so I had problems communicating with locals."

Since Karpov was an ethnic Russian who had a Russian passport, the Russian embassy arranged to pay for his trial expenses. Claiming that Karpov was being unfairly prosecuted, the Russian Ministry of Foreign Affairs complained that the Estonian prosecutors were not complying with international law.

"It is clear," a Ministry spokesman said, "That Estonia's political and judicial system can still sentence a person whose innocence is beyond doubt."[90]

Although Karpov was found guilty, the Estonian court gave him a suspended sentence and issued a fine. Despite the lenient sentence, the lead Estonian prosecutor on the case, Enia Ulviste, was satisfied with the result.

"We believe justice was done," she said, "He was at least forced to face his accusers."[91]

As the Estonian war crime trials continued, the Russian media contended that the proceedings were cruel because the Estonian prosecutors had indicted defendants who were

---

90   Stepanov, "Security Officer Sentenced."

91   Tarm, "Stalin Agent Found Guilty."

elderly and in poor health.[92] The Russian press also complained that the Estonian court system was trying to rewrite history and only wanted to exact revenge.

One defendant, Vladimir Pennart, took his complaint against the Estonian war crime trials to the European Court of Human Rights. Although Pennart received a suspended sentence for murdering three Estonian partisans in 1953 and 1954, [93] he, along with two other defendants, argued that they were wrongly convicted because the Estonian courts retroactively defined what constituted a crime. After reviewing the case, the European Court ruled that the execution of Estonian civilians could still be judged to be a crime against humanity even if the killings were considered lawful under Soviet law.

While the Estonian courts were able to convict several dozen defendants of war crimes, most of those who planned and carried out the deportations were never brought to trial. While the European Court of Human Rights confirmed that the abuses committed by the Soviets during their occupations were indeed crimes, the Soviet Union honored those who assisted the Baltic deportations as heroes, awarding medals to 8,850 Soviet troops and 635 Soviet security officers for the bravery they showed while they deported citizens from Estonia, Latvia, and Lithuania.[94]

According to Russian officials, there was no legal justification to assert that war crimes were committed in

---

92   "Soviet Deportations from Estonia," Wikipedia.

93   Liivoja, "Soviet War Crimes in the Baltic States."

94   "Operation Priboi," Wikipedia.

Estonia since the citizens of the Baltic state had voluntarily chosen to become part of the Soviet Union based on the elections that were held in the summer of 1940. The Russian leaders further argued that the Red Army forces entered Estonia, Latvia, and Lithuania with the consent of the three Baltic governments.

When Soviet troops returned in 1944, the Soviets contended they did so to liberate these countries from the Nazis.[95],[96] Once the Baltic states chose to join the Soviet Union, the Soviets argued that there could be no grounds for defining any Soviet activities as war crimes.

By the time I visited Estonia in the fall of 2018, there were few reminders of the brutal fighting that took place across the country during World War II. Tartu, the town where my brother, Michael, lives was heavily damaged in 1941 and then again in 1944. During their retreat at the end of the war, the German army destroyed many of the multi-story buildings that bordered the Emajõgi River while Soviet air attacks left the city's historic center in rubbles.

More than seventy years later, tree-lined parks filled the spaces where commercial and residential structures once stood. Older stucco buildings and wood-framed houses commingled with the glass-fronted storefronts and towering high-rises that sprawled along the river. When my mother returned to Estonia in the late 1990s for Michael's wedding, she was impressed by how vibrant Tartu had become with its outdoor cafes, bustling restaurants, and spanking modern buildings.

---

95   "Occupation of the Baltic States," Wikipedia.

96   Mälksoo, "Soviet Genocide?"

But where, she asked, was the rest of the town and the parts of the city she used to know?

When I visited my brother two decades later, I was impressed by the ways in which relics from Tartu's complex history could be found throughout the town. In one park, a statue of Gustav II Adolf, the Swedish king who established the University of Tartu in 1632, stared confidently at the horizon not far from a bustling town square filled with retail stores and restaurants. Close by, the remnants from a massive red brick cathedral built by the Germans in the thirteenth century overlooked the postwar buildings that housed the sprawling University of Tartu with its thirteen thousand students.[97]

Despite Tartu's peaceful ambiance, I was aware that scars from the war were not far from the surface. Records show that during the war 1,964 German soldiers were buried in unmarked graves in the Pauluse Kalmistu Cemetery. While other cemeteries devoted to those who died during the war are located throughout Estonia, not all the soldiers who were killed found their way to formal burial sites. Michael told me about an apartment building where the managers were forced to rebury a long dead German soldier whose moldering remains were discovered when they started to repave a parking lot.

In recent years, the German War Graves Commission has sponsored efforts to exhume, identify, and rebury the German casualties of the war who were killed on battle fields or in

---

97   The University of Tartu. https://ut.ee/en

prisoner of war camps throughout Eastern Europe and Russia. Since 1991 the Commission has arranged for 827,812 bodies to be reburied, yet the gravediggers have only been able to identify a third of the exhumed World War II corpses before giving them a proper burial.

In Viljandi, the War Graves Commission sponsored a project in which the bodies of seven hundred German soldiers were reburied. Prior to Estonia becoming independent, the Soviets demolished the grave markers that designated where German soldiers were buried and left the hillside cemetery unmarked and unnoticed.

To honor the fallen soldiers, the War Graves Commission hired local contractors to recover their corpses and to catalogue the names of the deceased based on the metal dog tags the German soldiers were required to wear. Once the crews identified as many soldiers as possible, the Commission erected a memorial wall that paid tribute to the war dead who were buried at the site, listing their names as well as their dates of birth and when they died.

For their part, the Soviets erected a Bronze Soldier memorial in 1947 to honor the Red Army soldiers who died during the war, but the statue was relocated from the Tallinn city center after Estonia became an independent state.

In addition to these memorials, other World War II sites have been preserved in Estonia. A prison used by the Soviets in Tartu has become the KGB Cells Museum, yet other detention sites have either been torn down or repurposed. The site of the Kuperjanov Barracks where Bruno was imprisoned can only be identified by four posts that formerly held up the roof of the building.

As Michael and I walked through Tartu's tree-lined neighborhoods, we passed by the red brick, two-story structure that is currently home to the Estonian Students' Society (ESS), the fraternity that Bruno joined while he attended the University of Tartu. The history of the turn-of-the century-building dates from 1920 when diplomats from Estonia and the Soviet Union gathered at the site to sign the Treaty of Tartu that first established Estonia as an independent state. The ESS fraternity's banner also served as the template for what became Estonia's blue, black, and white national flag.

After Estonia's War of Independence, sixty-three ESS students and alumni were awarded the country's Cross of Liberty for their bravery.[98] Any effort to honor members of the fraternity for their heroism during World War II would have been difficult while Estonia was occupied by the Soviet Union at the end of the war. Those ESS brothers who were part of Bruno's resistance network who survived the war would have needed to keep their subversive activities a secret for more than fifty years or face the ire of the Soviet courts.

In the 1960s, the Soviets held two public war crimes trials to accuse Estonians who collaborated with the Germans of committing crimes against humanity. During the Tartu trial, Soviet prosecutors charged three Estonians with murdering twelve thousand people at the Tartu concentration camp.

Two of the defendants, Ervin Viks and Karl Linnas, were convicted and sentenced to death in absentia while the third, Juhan Jüriste, was executed for his crimes. Twenty-five years after the trial concluded, the United States extradited Karl

---

98   Estonian Students' Society." Wikipedia.

Linnas to the Soviet Union where he later died in a Soviet prison hospital.[99]

As part of their efforts to uncover Nazi war crimes, the Soviets convened a Mass Crimes Investigation Commission. In Tartu at the Jakala trench, where Bruno was executed, the Soviet Commission arranged for workers to search for evidence that showed the scope of the executions that occurred at the site.

The workers discovered that before their retreat, the Germans attempted to cover up the remains of the prisoners who were killed at the trench. According to historical records, Nazi commanders ordered Polish and Czech prisoners from the Narva concentration camp to burn the corpses that could still be seen in the ravine. After their work was completed, the convict laborers were shot, and the German soldiers then burned their bodies to eliminate any evidence regarding the executions that occurred.

During the Soviet investigation into the Jakala Trench, workers uncovered the remains of 168 victims and then reburied their bodies in a common grave located in the town of Raadi. In honor of those who were executed, the Soviet Commission installed a flat stone marker that read, "People, be vigilant, here the Fascists killed 12,000 people."

Although no official listings have enumerated the names of those killed at the site, more current estimates suggest four thousand prisoners died at the Jakala Trench from the summer

---

99   "War Crimes Trials in Soviet Estonia," Wikiwand.

of 1941 through the spring of 1942. [100] During my 2018 visit, Michael, and I were unable to locate the trench. Nor could we find the stone marker that the Soviets had installed. But several years later, Michael connected with a colleague who was able to guide him to the historic ravine.

When he visited the trench, Michael said it was hard to identify where the ravine began and where it ended. Over the course of eighty years, the site had become overgrown with bushes, weeds, and fallen tree trunks. Some parts of the trench were heavily wooded while other areas had been converted into farmland. Much of the former execution site was covered with dirt and debris.

---

100 Puttsepp, "People Killed at the Tartu Concentration Camp."

Scene from what was once the Jakala Trench outside of Tartu

Many anonymous execution sites, like the Jakala Trench, continue to be unacknowledged. Aside from my mother's family, few know that this former anti-tank trench was the spot where Bruno Kulgma lost his life, along with several thousand other prisoners who were executed under orders from the Germans who were occupying Estonia. Like many Estonians who ended up being buried in unmarked graves far from their homes, these victims remain largely forgotten, a tragic reminder of the twisted justice system imposed on Estonia during World War II in which innocent people were judged to be guilty and those who were heroes were labelled as traitors.

CHAPTER 19

RECOVERING THE LOST PAST

According to one estimate, Estonia had a population of 1,128,000 residents in 1939 when World War II began.[101] By the time the war was over, one in four of the nation's citizens would be gone. [102] Tens of thousands of Estonians were deported, while others were executed or killed in battle. In addition, an estimated eighty thousand Estonians fled from their country, rather than live under Soviet control.[103] My mother and her family were among them.

When the Germans prepared to leave Estonia in September of 1944, their departure plans were rushed and chaotic since Hitler delayed giving his troops permission to retreat until it became clear they might soon be overrun. In the short amount of time available before the imminent arrival of the Red Army, the German military officers struggled to

---

101 "Demographics of Estonia," Wikipedia.

102 "Estonia in World War II," Wikipedia.

103 Lestal, "Remembering Estonia's WWII refugees."

evacuate fifty thousand troops, twenty thousand civilians, and one thousand Soviet prisoners of war along with thirty thousand tons of military equipment.[104]

As Estonians watched the signs that the Germans would soon be retreating, thousands tried to hire boats to travel to Sweden or Germany. The overseas trip across the churning waters of the Baltic Sea was perilous. Knowing the risks the Vares family faced, my grandfather sent my mother to Tallinn, instructing her to find any possible ways that would allow the Vares family to escape.

One crisp fall day in mid September, Mom was walking through Tallinn's market square when she ran into a German officer she had come to know. They were friends, she claimed, an acquaintance she must have met through her connections with Ernst Keitel. Years later, Mom did not remember his name, but he was apparently well connected enough to tell her that he would soon be leaving at the end of the week with the rest of the German army.

"When he saw how alarmed I was, he offered to help me and my family get on one of the German transport ships," Mom explained.

"He even said he could send a truck over to the apartment where we were staying to make sure we could get our luggage to the harbor."

When I asked my mother to describe him, she said he was in his mid-twenties, not what you would call dashing, but handsome in his own way. She also recalled that he was polite

---

104 "Tallinn Offensive," Wikipedia.

and reserved. "Just a nice guy," was the way she remembered him.

When he invited Mom to his apartment later that evening, she said she was happy to accept his invitation. Her memories from the rest of that long-ago evening were fuzzy. After they enjoyed some rich food and champagne, they talked about the war and shared their hopes for what their lives might become after the fighting finally ended.

"We were both young," she remembered. "And we talked about what all the young people at that time were worried about."

When I asked whether he tried to take advantage of how grateful she was for his help, she laughed. Their meeting was innocent, she protested. Although she did admit that as the night wore on, he became a bit amorous.

"What does that mean?" I asked.

Looking over her shoulder, she smiled while continuing to insist nothing happened.

"Did he just walk you back to the apartment where you were staying?"

"Not quite," she said, "When he leaned over to kiss me, I'm afraid I had to run to the bathroom where I got sick to my stomach and that ended that."

More than sixty years later, my mother merely said the situation was awkward and embarrassing. Whatever might have transpired, the officer kept his promise and early the next morning, on September 21, 1944, a German army truck arrived to pick up my mother and her family as well as the trunks they planned to carry with them.

"When we got to the harbor, it was packed," Mom recalled, "We were surrounded by people who were desperate to escape because everyone knew the Soviets would be arriving within the next several days. When my father noticed that one of the boats had Red Cross markings, he asked our driver to steer toward that loading dock because he thought he could help, but there were long lines of wounded soldiers waiting to get on board, so the driver took us to another ship."

Mom knew that she and her family were lucky to have a German soldier who could guide them as they boarded one of the troop transport ships. A few hours later when the German sailors pulled up the ship gangplanks, the frantic Estonians who were waiting on the docks cried out in desperation. When some of the passengers started to sing the Estonian national anthem, Mom said all she could think about was how relieved she was to finally leave Estonia.

"The next morning," Mom said, "The sky was clear, and I decided to go up to one of the ship's observation towers where I started talking with some German sailors. When they spotted a squadron of Soviet bombers heading toward the ships in the German convoy, everyone on the boat started to panic because there was no place where we could take cover."

Mom never admitted that she was afraid of dying on that day. While the others around her began to scream, she said, all she could do was just numbly watch as the planes drew closer. One of my mother's Estonian friends, Miriam, who was also a passenger on the same ship, described her desperation, as the planes drew closer.

"I was standing next to my sister on one of the decks and there was no place for us to hide. When the bombs started to drop, I turned my head and then an instant later some shrapnel hit my sister. One minute she was there, and the next minute she was dead."

Selma, another Estonian, remembered the thundering sound that shook the boats when the bombs started to fall. Shortly after the aerial attack began, she was horrified when she looked at the nearby hospital ship, the Moero, and saw that its bow was staring to tilt toward the sky.

Mom described the chaotic scene as the ship passengers watched the Moero slowly sink over the next hour. Desperate to survive, the passengers who had been on board the hospital ship flung themselves into the frigid Baltic waters and then cried out to be rescued. The thousands of wounded soldiers who remained on the lower decks had fewer options.[105]

Fifty-five minutes after it was hit, the Moero disappeared into the Baltic Sea. The attack occurred twenty-six miles south of the Latvian port of Ventspils. Only six hundred passengers were rescued, while twenty-seven hundred died after the ship was sunk.[106]

"All I could think about as I watched the Red Cross boat go down was how easily my family and I could have been among the passengers who died," Mom said, "We were all in shock as we watched the hospital ship sink."

Only a few hours later, the Soviet planes returned, but this time they missed their targets. After enduring the aerial attacks, the German transport ships continued onward, and finally reached the harbor of Danzig at the end of the day.

Sobered by my mother's close escape, I said, "You must have been relieved when you knew that you were finally safe."

---

105 Kissa, *Pilgrimage*, 139.

106 Wreck Site, "MV Moero, 1944."

Mom laughed darkly, "After that day, I'm not sure I ever felt completely safe."

When the German ships docked in Danzig, Mom said the harbor town was teeming with refugees. Rather than fight the crowds that were streaming toward the railway station, my grandfather decided to wait a day before trying to buy train tickets. The family's plan was to travel to Berlin and then to continue south to Mühlau in southeast Germany where they planned to stay with my grandfather's cousin, Mari.

After some German sailors invited my mother to go with them to find a pub, she readily agreed. Mom was eager to get off the boat and enthusiastic about exploring Danzig.

"After we found a bar near the harbor, we were just finishing our first round of drinks, when the air raid sirens began blasting," she recalled.

"Everyone dropped to the floor and scrambled under the tables while the bartender turned off the lights and the room became pitch black. At first, we could hear bombs dropping in other parts of the city. Then there was just a deadly silence. I can't even remember how long we had to wait, but it seemed like forever before we heard the all-clear signal, and we could run back to the ship."

When I asked what she remembered most from that time, Mom said, "The worst feeling was not knowing what was going to happen. We felt so helpless. We couldn't be sure whether we might be the next ones who were killed."

Throughout the war, my mother heard the reports about the millions of people who were losing their lives. Young men were dying in battle while scores of civilians were being killed as bombing raids devastated cities and town across Europe.

Remembering that distant past, she said, "I can't tell you why we were so lucky. It was really a miracle that we were able to leave Estonia and thank God we were not on that hospital ship when it sank. When you watch people die, you know that you can never take anything for granted. It was a lesson I learned the hard way."

The next day Mom and her family travelled to Mühlau, a sleepy German town located in southeast Germany near the border with Czechoslovakia. The trip was long, but Mom remembered that each mile took her family further away from the intense fighting that was happening along the Eastern Front.

"As you can imagine, we were enormously relieved when we finally made it to Mari's house. It still amazes me when I remember that the trains in Germany were running on time. Then a day after we arrived—can you believe in the middle of the war—our trunks were delivered to Mari's house."

As Mom and her family settled in to wait, they believed it would be only a matter of a few months before the war would end and they could go back to Estonia. Nobody expected that their stay in Mühlau would last until the following spring.

Mom After her Arrival in Mühlau, Germany, Fall of 1944

Despite the progress that the Allied forces were making both on the Eastern and the Western fronts, Hitler refused to believe that his German army would be defeated. Even though his forces were overextended, outnumbered, and running short of weapons and supplies, the German chancellor insisted that the Nazi army should continue to fight.

As they watched the war drag on month after month, Mom and her family recognized they were becoming unwelcome guests in Mari's small house.

"There we were, the four of us, my parents, my brother, and me crowded into just a few rooms with Mari and her husband. As the winter set in, Mari worried constantly about her sons who were fighting with the German army. Peter was stationed somewhere in Russia while Wolfgang was in Italy. I just tried to get out of the house whenever I could."

The winter of 1944-45 was colder than usual. Food was scarce and most Germans struggled to keep their homes heated. As bleak news filtered in from the frontlines, Hitler announced that he had a secret plan to win the war, a boast few believed particularly when the German army began conscripting teenage boys and elderly men.

To stiffen the resolve of German citizens, Nazi news media cautioned what might happen if the Soviets occupied German soil. Posters warned that "Bolshevism means slavery, rape, mass murder, and extermination – fight back! Fight until victory!" [107] German news outlets also circulated graphic pictures that showed the brutalized bodies of women and children who were alleged to have been raped and murdered by Soviet soldiers in the town of Nemmersdorf.

After the start of the new year, the Allied bombing raids became more frequent and more lethal, as they struck cities and towns throughout Germany. While everyone in Mari's house anxiously worried over what might happen when the war ended, small quarrels broke out.

"I can't remember why we weren't getting along," Mom said. "Your grandmother wanted to help with the household chores, and as you know, her feelings could easily get hurt. As time went on, I think Mari just resented the fact that we had been staying with her for so long. We tried to keep out of her way, but there was no place we could go. We all just wanted the war to be over and the endless waiting got on our nerves. As the months wore on, I was really afraid that Mari would ask us to leave."

To escape the tension that was building in Mari's house, Mom started meeting with a Latvian friend to practice her English. Only months after leaving Estonia, she was already

---

107 Hardy, "The Nazi Propaganda."

preparing for the possibility that her future might not involve returning to her home country.

The massive bombing campaign that the Allied forces unleashed against Dresden in the spring of 1945 caught everyone by surprise. Located at the crossroads between several east-west railway lines, the city was swollen with nearly 750,000 refugees[108] and seemed to be an unlikely military target.

Late in the evening of February 13, more than eight hundred British aircraft thundered across the sky to begin what would become a three-day aerial bombardment. After the squadrons dropped tons of heavy explosives and incendiary bombs, the horizon around Dresden lit up, as white-hot flames rose fifteen thousand feet into the air in a blaze of light that could be seen more than fifty miles away in Mühlau.

The next day the eastern horizon glowed with a reddish hue. As the bombing raids on Dresden continued, two thousand U.S. Air Force bombers dropped additional explosives on the beleaguered city. By the time the campaign was over, thirteen square miles of the town had been obliterated and twenty-five thousand civilians were killed.[109]

"We could hear the planes thundering overhead and knew the bombers were heading east," Mom remembered. "It was only later that we learned how devastating the attack on Dresden had been."

During the following weeks, the relentless aerial campaign continued as Allied bombers targeted Chemnitz, a city located

---

108 Taylor, "How Many Died in the Bombing of Dresden?"

109 Taylor, "How Many Died in the Bombing of Dresden?"

ten miles away from Mühlau. As dark sooty clouds drifted across the sky from the bombing raids, Mom could only hope that the war would soon end.

Only a month later, she was listening to a BBC radio report when she learned that the American army had crossed over the Rhine River for the first time. Encountering little resistance, the U.S. Third Army under General George Patton continued their advance and reached Germany's far eastern border a few weeks later.

As the U.S. Army troop trucks were drawing close to Mühlau, the town's residents dangled white pillowcases and sheets from their windows to signal their surrender. For her part, Mom was thrilled.

"When the U.S. Army jeeps started rolling into town, I cheered since I knew the war was finally over. Mari and her German neighbors were more cautious because they were worried about how they might be treated. Of course, for them, the end of the war meant defeat."

Even though General Patton and the American soldiers he commanded were eager to keep advancing toward Berlin, General Dwight Eisenhower ordered them to hold their positions. Anticipating that the final battle in Berlin would be bloody, the American Commander decided to allow the Soviet army to be the first forces that would fight for the German capitol. Taking advantage of the break, the battle-hardened G.I.s handed out chocolate bars and chewing gum to the town's children before heading to the local tavern to celebrate.

Mom remembered how young and friendly the American G.I.s were.

"There were lots of soldiers milling around and I started talking with a couple of them. I was so excited that the Americans had arrived, and the soldiers were happy as well. They knew that the fighting was almost over and soon they would be returning home."

"It was like New Year's Eve. People were dancing in the streets, kissing, and hugging. When you live through wartime, you start to realize that life can be short, and you want to make the most of it. We partied for days especially after we heard that Hitler was dead, and we could finally believe that Germany would stop fighting."

During the celebrations, Mom met an American G.I. who became her friend.

"He was attractive, and we enjoyed spending time together, but we had only been seeing each other for a week when his unit got orders to move west so the Soviets could take control over the area around Mühlau."

When Winston Churchill, Franklin Roosevelt, and Joseph Stalin met in Yalta earlier in the year, the Allied leaders determined that the Elbe River would be designated as the western border for the Soviet Occupation Zone. In keeping with the agreement, Patton and his troops were ordered to move back to the sector of Germany that would be occupied by the Americans while the Soviets took over the territory that included Mühlau and other nearby towns.

While the G.I.s were loading their transport trucks to begin their withdrawal, the Soviet Army demanded that any German soldiers who tried to surrender to the Americans should instead be turned over to the Red Army. They also ordered that the Americans send all expatriates from the Baltic countries and other Soviet-controlled territories to a Soviet processing center that was being established in Chemnitz.

"You can imagine how desperate we were when we learned about the Soviet demands," Mom recalled. "Even though we wanted to go home, we did not want to return if the Soviets were going to be in control. When we first escaped, we really thought we were safe. Then months later, the Soviets arrived and began insisting that we had to be shipped back to Estonia. We were devastated and concerned about what might happen if we went back."

While the U.S. Army was packing up to leave, Mom appealed to her G.I. friend for help. However it was that he managed to arrange it, my mother, my grandparents, my uncle, and Mom's Latvian friend found themselves a day later seated in the back of an American troop carrier as it pulled out of Mühlau just a few hours before the Soviet troops arrived.

In film footage taken by G.I.s in the first few months after Germany surrendered, long lines of German soldiers can be seen walking along the country's highways with their hands in the air. Barren fields, demolished towns, and burned-out tanks littered the landscape as thousands of displaced families crowded the roads. They carried all their worldly possessions in suitcases as they trudged toward the refugee centers that the Allied nations had established.

Over the next day, the troop convoy carrying my mother and her family trundled over two hundred miles towards the headquarters of the American Occupation Zone in Frankfurt. When I asked what happened to the G.I. who had helped her, Mom said they lost touch.

"He left with the U.S. Third Army when they moved towards Berlin while my family and I ended up in Frankfurt.

There was no way we could send letters to each other. All I can say is that he came into my life when I needed help, and I will always be very grateful that he made sure my family and I stayed safe. While we were together, we were caught up in the excitement everyone felt when we knew the war was finally over. Then we ended up going our separate ways."

The G.I. who Helped my Mother and her
Family Travel to Frankfurt, May 1945

Later, as I was looking through my mother's wartime albums, I found a picture of her G.I. friend, whose name I discovered was Al. As he continued his stint with the U.S. Third Army, he most likely helped guard some of the 1,650,000 German soldiers who surrendered at the end of the war.[110] Like most American soldiers, he would have been eager

---

110 Cooper, The German Army, 529.

to return stateside to the world of peace and security that was waiting for him.

My mother's situation was less certain. After living through the horror of the war years, she was left with no passport, no country to call home and no clear hopes for the future. Yet, she had been lucky to survive and to find people who could help her.

When Mom was desperate to leave Estonia, a German soldier arranged for her family to join the retreating German army that left Tallinn harbor a day before the Soviets took control. Less than a year later, with help from an American G.I., Mom's family avoided a Soviet demand that they be repatriated. Instead, they boarded an American troop truck that was travelling to the American Occupation Zone in Frankfurt.

By a twist of fortune, Mom and her family avoided being passengers on the Moero, the hospital ship that was sunk by a squadron of Soviet planes. She survived a Soviet bombing raid in Danzig and watched in horror as the nearby towns of Dresden and Chemnitz were devastated in a series of Allied bombing attacks.

When my mother and her family arrived in Frankfurt, they had no way to know what their future might be, but they were safe, the war was over, and they could start to rebuild their lives. Mom ended up spending five years in Germany as a displaced person before she could find her way to the United States. Once again, she was helped by an American soldier, the man who became my father.

CHAPTER 20

LASTING SCARS FROM THE WAR

After hearing the stories other Estonians shared about the wartime experiences their families endured, I realized how fortunate my mother's fate had been. One family friend from Tallinn told me that she desperately wanted to escape before the Soviets occupied Estonia in the fall of 1944, but when she reached the harbor, she discovered that the German troop ships were already gone.

Another Estonian man, one of my mother's friends from the university, recounted how he hoped to stay in Finland after fighting with the Finnish army during the war, but under pressure from the Soviets, the Finns forced all Estonian soldiers to return to Estonia rather than allowing them to remain in Finland.

After the Soviets incorporated Estonia into the Soviet Union, many Estonians found that the options available to them were constrained and dissent was impossible. To stamp out any resistance, the Soviets implemented a second deportation in March of 1949 and transported twenty thousand Estonian men, women, and children to Siberia. The

Soviets also used the judicial system to prosecute Estonians, accusing them of crimes that were defined by the Soviet legal code. Between 1942 through 1990, the Soviet courts convicted thirty-seven thousand Estonians for activities that were labelled as undermining Soviet authority.

After Stalin died in 1953, the Soviets permitted thirty thousand Estonians to return from Siberia, but the former deportees remained under surveillance. Even though there was no evidence that they had committed any crimes, they had trouble finding housing, securing jobs, and continuing their studies. [111]

Yet, in defiance of the efforts by the Soviets to suppress the memories Estonians carried from the war, Estonian families preserved the memories of those relatives who died. They remembered grandparents who were executed and mourned the fathers and uncles who disappeared in prisoner of war camps. They also kept alive the names of the aunts and uncles, nieces and nephews who never returned from Siberia.

One Estonian I met during my travels described how his grandfather was shot by Nazi soldiers when he gave a "Heil Hitler" salute with two arms instead of one. Another recalled that his great-uncle was executed as a Communist because he once called out "Long live Stalin" at a community meeting, believing this would protect his family.

The narrative told by Mart Laar, a former Prime Minister of Estonia, demonstrated how easily Estonians could find

---

[111] Estonian State Commission. "Phase III: The Soviet Occupation of Estonia from 1944."

themselves caught between the Soviets and the Germans with both sides accusing Estonians of being traitors.

"My grandfather was shot by the Nazis," Mart wrote, "Two of my great-uncles were sent to Siberian death camps by the Soviets. My father-in-law was deported to Siberia as a nine-year-old boy where he struggled to survive against death by starvation. Unknown to him, his hopes of seeing his father alive again were in vain; his father was shot early in 1941 by the KGB in Moscow's Kirov prison."

In recent years, Estonians have sought to preserve a historical record of the country's experiences during World War II. In 2018, the Estonian Institute of Historical Memory erected a large granite memorial that listed the names of twenty-two thousand Estonians who were murdered, exiled, or forcibly resettled while the country was occupied between 1940 through 1991.

The Institute has also established an electronic database that contains information on more than one hundred thousand Estonians who were victims of Communism while a second virtual platform enumerates those who were victimized during the Nazi occupation. In a third database, the Institute has memorialized the tens of thousands of Estonians who fled from their homeland during World War II. Finally, Estonians from around the world can access the Institute's oral history portal, entitled *Collect our Story*, to upload video accounts of their family narratives.[112]

---

112 Eesti Mälu Instituut, Estonian Institute of Historical Memory.

This book represents my effort to document what happened to my mother and her family during World War II and to describe how they managed to survive. For my mother, remembering the past was painful, but she did not view herself as a victim, particularly after she created a new life as an American citizen.

During the five years while Mom was living as a displaced person in Frankfurt, Germany, she found work as a laboratory technician at a U.S. Army hospital where she practiced her English and honed her employment skills. When the U.S. Congress passed the Displaced Persons Act in 1948 that granted American visas to refugees from certain European countries, she applied for permission to immigrate to the United States.

During the previous year, she had been dating my father who was working at the U.S. Army hospital as a physician. During the war, Dad was drafted, rushed through medical school and then once he finished his medical training, stationed in Frankfurt in the fall of 1947. Even though Mom was spending much of her free time with my father, she was still pursuing her own plans to move to America.

"I knew I wanted to leave Europe and I was trying to find a way to get to the United States," she said, "After I heard the news that my visa application had been approved, I was all set to go. But I didn't know your father's intentions, so I asked him point blank whether he planned to marry me or not."

Dad remembered being happy that my mother's visa had been approved, but he was hesitant to make a commitment.

"Times were still hard," he said, "And I didn't know what kind of job I could find when I returned to the U.S." he said,

"But I still got down on one knee and asked your mother, 'Will you marry me?'"

She agreed, and six months later she moved with my father to Philadelphia where they started a family while Dad set up a family practice office in the basement of the townhome where we lived. After I was born, my two brothers and two sisters followed within the space of nine years.

While Mom was happy to have emigrated to the United States, she sometimes found it difficult to fit in.

"It was hard in the 1950s to be a foreigner and to be different. Few people could possibly understand what I had been through," she recalled. "Most didn't even know where Estonia was. They thought of me as a war bride, and I guess in a way that's what I was."

Not wanting to stand out, Mom explained that she tried to be more American than the rest.

"I was embarrassed by my accent, and I didn't want anyone to know that I had been a displaced person. It was so obvious that I was different, but no one brought it up. And if they asked, I didn't really want to explain."

After living through the war, Mom wanted to leave the past behind. The only time I recall her being sentimental about her former life was the one Christmas when she decided to show my two children how the holiday was celebrated in Estonia. As my family settled around a roaring fire, my father, who was dressed in a rented Santa Claus suit, knocked on the front door and amazed my two small children when he posed as Father Christmas and gave them small presents.

For our dinner, my mother prepared a traditional Estonian menu consisting of roast duck, blood sausage, beet salad, and pickled pumpkin, topped off by a meringue dessert. As we lingered around the table, a dozen candles in two bronze candelabras cast a warm glow on our contented faces, as wispy plumes of smoke curled through the air.

The smells from the kitchen, the crackling of the fire, and the looks of anticipation on my children's faces likely helped my mother to remember happier times when all the people she loved, including Asta and Bruno, gathered around her family's table. I wondered if the bright lights of the candles led her to recall how Estonians honored their deceased loved ones by placing candles on their graves during the Christmas holidays.

Throughout my childhood, my family never visited graveyards. Nor did we talk about our relatives who had passed away. Yet, I have always been curious about our unspoken connection to the people who came before us. My mother's Estonian identity was an essential part of the person she was. She was a stoic survivor who was determined to find a way to prosper, much like the generations of Estonians who preserved their ethnic identity for centuries while the country was occupied by foreign neighbors. As I gathered my family stories, I have come to appreciate and honor the courage of Estonians like Bruno who resisted the take-over of their country both during and after World War II. For me, theirs has become a story worth remembering and retelling.

In Germany, the country's leaders have initiated a program to pay tribute to those who were victimized by the Nazis. Across more than twelve hundred cities and towns throughout Europe and Russia, the Germans have installed more than seventy thousand small brass stumbling stones (*stolpersteine*). The plaques commemorate the names of those who were deported and killed while also identifying their last known residence. By creating a personalized memorial for each victim, the project assures that they will not be forgotten.[113]

Many of the organized remembrance projects in Estonia, Germany, and other parts of Europe have been inspired by this same goal. Acknowledging the names of those victims who were killed during World War II helps to underscore the barbarity of the war crimes that were committed while deepening the hope that such heinous acts will never be repeated.

Estonia has now been an independent country for more than thirty years. During this time, the small Baltic country has taken its place as a member of the European Union as well as becoming a participant in the NATO military alliance. Even though Bruno's name might not be remembered, I like to believe that he, along with the other patriots who resisted Estonia's occupation, laid a foundation for the decades long battle Estonians waged to keep their dream of independence alive. As a result of their stubborn determination, Estonia has become the vibrant, prosperous, and fiercely independent nation it is today.

While Estonians look toward the future, their country's past is never far behind. Near the center of Tartu, my brother lives in a two-story stucco house that was constructed during the postwar Soviet occupation. More than a dozen apple trees shade his expansive backyard. The lot, he told me, was once part of a larger estate owned by a German landlord who divided up the property when Estonia became independent in the early 1920s.

---

113 Apperly, "'Stumbling Stones.'"

When the Estonian owner of the property disappeared during the war, a local family obtained permission to use the land to build a house. Several decades later after Estonia regained its independence, the building occupants filed an application to claim ownership of the house they had constructed as well as the land on which it had been built. Their claim was not contested by anyone who had previously owned the lot.

When I heard the story, I was haunted by the ephemeral presence of the family who once owned the property and then disappeared. How many other Estonians, I wondered, were deported, displaced, or killed during the war and then never returned to lay claim to their former homes or to their national heritage?

My mother's story is one of stubborn resilience, but it is also a story of luck and of finding help from the right people at the right time. While there is no doubt that Mom was courageous, she could not have succeeded without having fortune on her side. As I compiled Bruno's story, I could see that he was brave as well. Yet, he ended up encountering a different set of challenges, ones that despite his best efforts, he could not overcome.

I know that I am who I am because of my Estonian past and the relatives, both known and unknown, who came before me. I am also the person I was able to become because of my mother's wartime experiences and her strong motivation to survive and prosper in the new life she adopted.

As part of my Christmas Eve traditions, I have begun lighting candles to remember those who have gone before me. The bright flames remind me of the courage that helped members of my family face the challenges before them while the dripping wax underscores how quickly the light that represents our individual gifts can be extinguished. After the candles are snuffed out, I watch the smoke that circles around me and remind myself that the memory of those we have loved never fully disappears.

The life I have known has always been safe and secure. By contrast, my parents lived through a time when war devasted the world around them and killed many of those they knew and loved. Their experiences led them to become stubbornly self-reliant, the traits they wanted their children to share. I have inherited a legacy of strength and determination, of courage and self-sacrifice, and of an enduring commitment to honor my Estonian background.

History, it is said, has a way of repeating itself. Perhaps war will always be with us. Perhaps as well, there will always be the stories of patriotic heroes, like Bruno, who died so that freedom can live, democracies can prosper, and the world, as we know it, can be a better place.

Bibliography

"1940 Estonian Parliamentary Election." Wikipedia.
    Accessed February 10, 2019. https://en.wikipedia.org/
    wiki/1940_Estonian_parliamentary_election.

"1991 Soviet Coup d'Etat Attempt." Wikipedia. Accessed
    April 3, 2019. https://en.wikipedia.org/wiki/1991_
    Soviet_coup_d%27%C3%A9tat_attempt.

"Air Warfare of World War II." Wikipedia. Accessed May
    20, 2020. https://en.wikipedia.org/wiki/Air_warfare_
    of_World_War_II.

Altau, Karl. "Remembering the Deadly Baltic Deportations."
    Dissident, June 23, 2015. Accessed October 6, 2020.
    http://blog.victimsofcommunism.org/remembering-
    the-deadly-baltic-deportations.

Apperly, Eliza, "'Stumbling Stones': a Different Vision of
    Holocaust Remembrance." *The Guardian*, February
    18, 2019. https://www.theguardian.com/cities/2019/
    feb/18/stumbling-stones-a-different-vision-of-
    holocaust-remembrance.

"Arnold Meri." Wikipedia. Accessed February 20, 2019.
    https://en.wikipedia.org/wiki/Arnold_Meri.

Berendson, Risto. "The Deportee Rejects the Charges."
    Eesti Päevaleht, March 23, 1998. Accessed July 19,

2019. https://epl.delfi.ee/eesti/kuuditaja-torjub-suudistusi?id=50753168.

Berger, Joseph. "Some in Estonia Greeted Nazis in '41 as Liberators." The New York Times, April 22, 1987. https://www.nytimes.com/1987/04/22/world/some-in-estonia-greeted-nazis-in-41-as-liberators.html

Birn, Ruth Betinna. "Collaboration with Nazi Germany in Eastern Europe: The Case of the Estonian Security Police." *Contemporary European History*, 10 no. 2, (July 2001): 181-198. Accessed August 7, 2020. https://www.jstor.org/stable/20081785?read-now=1&seq=14#page_scan_tab_contents

Bultar, Prit. *Between Giants: The Battle for the Baltics in World War II*, (Osprey Publishing, 2013). Accessed December 24, 2019. https://books.google.com/books?id=VFqICwAAQBAJ&pg=PT36&lpg=PT36&dq=karl+selter+molotov&source=bl&ots=zPtsdICwhy&sig=ACfU3U0ghMgPcRDwoX28h-XZUxkKjGkqFg&hl=en&sa=X&ved=2ahUKEwjpjsCG0ofgAhWiMXwKHQVuAX8Q6AEwDnoECAEQAQ#v=onepage&q=karl%20selter%20molotov&f=false.

Burds, Jeffrey. "Collaborators, the German Occupation and Stalin's NKVD, 1941-1943," *East European Politics & Societies*, 32, no. 3 (August 2018): 606-638.

Bush, Robert D. "An Investigation into the Trial of a Nazi War Criminal: Joachim Von Ribbentrop at Nuremberg, Germany, 1945-1946." University of Richmond, UR Scholarship Repository, 1963. Accessed March 27, 2019. https://www.upi.com/Archives/1946/09/30/Profiles-of-the-21-Nazi-leaders-on-trial-at-Nuremberg/2178534120119/.

"Castrop, Rauxel, Chemnitz, Colberg, Cologne/Koln, Cottbus and Cuxhaven," Accessed March 20, 2019. http://www.exulanten.com/bombb2.html.

"Chemnitz." Wikipedia. Accessed March 20, 2019 https://en.wikipedia.org/wiki/Chemnitz.

Chivers, C.J. "Cousin of Former Estonian President Charged with Genocide." *The New York Times*, (August 22, 2007). Accessed February 21, 2019. https://www.nytimes.com/2007/08/22/world/europe/22iht-estonia.4.7214101.html.

"Commissar Order." Wikipedia. Accessed September 22, 2021. https://en.wikipedia.org/wiki/Commissar_Order.

Communist Crimes, "The Destruction of the Estonian Political Elite during the Soviet Occupation in 1940-1941." Accessed May 12, 2021. https://communistcrimes.org/en/destruction-estonian-political-elite-during-soviet-occupation-1940-1941.

Cooper, Matthew. *The German Army, 1933-1945*, (Lanham, MD: Scarborough House, 1978).

"Demographics of Estonia." Wikipedia. Accessed October 19, 2020. https://en.wikipedia.org/wiki/Demographics_of_Estonia.

"Displaced Persons Camps in Post-World War II Europe." Wikipedia. Accessed June 28,2021. https://en.wikipedia.org/wiki/Displaced_persons_camps_in_post%E2%80%93World_War_II_Europe#:~:text=At%20the%20end%20of%20the,and%20Jewish%20concentration%2Dcamp%20survivors.

Earl, Hilary. "Good Nazis and Other Germans: The Fate of SS Einsatzgruppen Commander Martin Sandberger in Postwar Germany." Accessed January 15, 2019. https://www.academia.edu/6022173/Good_Nazis_and_Other_Germans_The_fate_of_SS-Einsatzgruppen_Commander_Martin_Sandberger_in_postwar_Germany,

Eesti Mälu Instituut. Estonian Institute of Historical Memory. Accessed November 15, 2022. https://mnemosyne.ee/en/

Eesti Päevaleht. "Primadonna Was Arrested on the Last Day of the Year." December 19, 1998. Accessed August 15, 2021. https://epl.delfi.ee/artikkel/50766217/primadonna-vahistati-aasta-viimasel-paeval

Ellman, Michael and S. Maksudov. "Soviet Deaths in the Great Patriotic War: A Note." *Europe-Asia Studies*, 46, no. 4. (1994): 671-680. https://www.jstor.org/stable/152934.

ERR.EE News. "June 1941: Soviet Authorities Arrest and Deport 95,000." June 14, 2017. Accessed September 19, 2018. https://news.err.ee/602033/june-1941-soviet-authorities-arrest-and-deport-95-000.

Estonian International Commission on the Investigation of Crimes Against Humanity. "Phase II: The German Occupation of Estonia in 1941-1944." Accessed July 28, 2019. http://www.mnemosyne.ee/hc.ee/pdf/conclusions_en_1941-1944.pdf.

Estonian International Commission for the Investigation of Crimes Against Humanity. "Phase 1: The Soviet Occupation of Estonia in 1940-41." Accessed July 21, 2020. http://www.mnemosyne.ee/hc.ee/pdf/conclusions_en_1940-1941.pdf.

Estonian International Commission for the Investigation of Crimes Against Humanity. "Phase III: The Soviet Occupation of Estonia from 1944." Accessed January 12, 2023. https://mnemosyne.ee/wp-content/uploads/2021/12/conclusions_en_1944-.pdf.

"Estonia in World War II." Wikipedia. Accessed July 20, 2019. https://en.wikipedia.org/wiki/Estonia_in_World_War_II.

Estonian State Commission on Examination of the Politics of Repression. "The White Book: Losses Inflicted on the Estonian Nation by Occupation Regimes 1940-1991." Accessed February 17, 2019. https://www.riigikogu.ee/wpcms/wp-content/uploads/2015/02/TheWhiteBook.pdf.

"Estonian Students' Society." Wikipedia. Accessed September 30, 2020. https://en.wikipedia.org/wiki/Estonian_Students%27_Society.

Estonia World. "Estonia Remembers the Soviet Deportations." June 14, 2021. Accessed August 20, 2021. https://estonianworld.com/life/estonia-remembers-the-soviet-deportations/.

"Falsifiers of History." Wikipedia. Accessed January 21, 2019. https://en.wikipedia.org/wiki/Falsifiers_of_History.

"Guerilla War in the Baltic States." Wikipedia. Accessed January 12, 2023 https://en.wikipedia.org/wiki/Guerrilla_war_in_the_Baltic_states.

Hardy, Denise and Marta Kasztelan. "The Nazi Propaganda that Triggered a Mass Suicide." OZY. Accessed June 2, 2021. https://www.ozy.com/true-and-stories/the-nazi-propaganda-that-triggered-a-mass-suicide/363867/.

"Heinrich Bergmann (SS Member)." Wikipedia. Accessed January 6, 2019. https://de.wikipedia.org/wiki/ Heinrich_Bergmann_(SS-Mitglied).

Hiio, Toomas. "World War II: Military Operations and Units, Military Government and Agencies." Accessed July 19, 2020. http://muuseum.viljandimaa.ee/vana/ aastaraamat/2011_toim_2/hiio.pdf.

Hirsh, Francine. "The Soviets at Nuremberg: International Law, Propaganda, and the Making of the Postwar Order." *The American Historical Review*, 113, no. 3, (June 2008): 701-730. https://www.jstor.org/ stable/30223049?read-now=1&seq=19#page_scan_ tab_contents.

"History of the Jews in Estonia." Wikipedia. Accessed September 15, 2021. https://en.wikipedia.org/wiki/ History_of_the_Jews_in_Estonia.

"Idel Jakobson." Wikipedia. Accessed February 17, 2019. https://et.wikipedia.org/wiki/Idel_Jakobson.

Jewish Virtual Library. "The Einsatzgruppen: Report by Einsatzgruppe A in the Baltic Countries." October 15, 1941. Accessed September 15, 2021. https://www. jewishvirtuallibrary.org/report-by-einsatzgruppe-a- in-the-baltic-countries-october-1941.

Kaitsepolitseiamet. "Judicial Decisions." Accessed July19, 2019. https://www.kapo.ee/en/content/judicial-decisions.html.

"Karl Selter." Wikipedia. Accessed January 24, 2019. https://en.wikipedia.org/wiki/Karl_Selter.

Kay, Alex J. "Transition to Genocide, July 1941: Einsatzkommando 9 and the Annihilation of Soviet Jewry." Accessed September 24, 2021. https://academic.oup.com/hgs/article-abstract/27/3/411/766645

Kelam, Mari-Ann and Heiki Ahonen. "Chronology of Selected Estonian Events, 1986-1988. Accessed April 3, 2019. https://truecostmovie.com/img/TSR/pages/section_06/1986-1988_Chronology_of_Selected_Estonian_Events.pdf.

Kissa, Selma. *Pilgrimage, a Novel.* (College Station, Texas: Virtualbookworm.com. 2005).

Kung, Andres. *Communism in the Baltic States.* Jarl Hjalmarson Foundation, 2008. Accessed August 23, 2020. https://www.hjalmarsonfoundation.se/wp-content/uploads/2011/12/Communism-in-the-Baltic-States.pdf.

Laar, Mart. *Estonia in World War II.* Tallinn: Grenader, 2005.

Laar, Mart. *The Forgotten War, Armed Resistance Movement in Estonia in 1944-1956.* Tallinn: Grenader, 2005.

Laar, Mart. *Red Terror. Repressions of the Soviet Occupation Authorities in Estonia.* Grenader, 2005.

"Lennart Meri." Wikipedia. Accessed January 30, 2019. https://en.wikipedia.org/wiki/Lennart_Meri.

Lestal, Tania. "Remembering Estonia's WWII Refugees," *Estonian World,* (September 19, 2019). Accessed October 5, 2020. https://estonianworld.com/life/remembering-estonias-wwii-refugees//.

Liivoja, Rain, "Competing Histories, Soviet War Crimes in the Baltic States." Accessed October 10, 2021. https://oxford.universitypressscholarship.com/view/10.1093/acprof:oso/9780199671144.001.0001/acprof-9780199671144-chapter-12.

Liivoja Rain. "Soviet War Crimes in the Baltic States," *The Hidden Histories of War Crimes Trials,* translators. Kevin Heller and Gerry Simpson, Chapter 12. Accessed February 10, 2019. http://www.oxfordscholarship.com/view/10.1093/acprof:oso/9780199671144.001.0001/acprof-9780199671144-chapter-12.

"List of Countries by Population in 1939." Wikipedia. Accessed June 19, 2020. https://en.wikipedia.org/wiki/List_of_countries_by_population_in_1939.

Lithuanian Quarterly Journal of Arts and Sciences. "Minutes of the Soviet-Estonian Negotiations for the Mutual Pact of 1939." Volume 14, No. 2, (Summer 1968). Accessed April 20, 2021. http://lituanus.org/1968/68_2_03Doc4.html.

Luck, David. "Use and Abuse of Holocaust Documents: Reitlinger and "How Many?" *Jewish Social Studies,* vol. 41, no. 2. Accessed September 29, 2021. https://www.jstor.org/stable/4467046.

Mälksoo, Lauri. "Soviet Genocide? Communist Mass Deportations in the Baltic States and International Law." *Leiden Journal of International Law,* 14(4) (December 2001): 757-787. Accessed July 14, 2019. https://www.cambridge.org/core/journals/leiden-journal-of-international-law/article/abs/soviet-genocide-communist-mass-deportations-in-the-baltic-states-and-international-law/FAB5F421076CFD31803523496AB47722

Maripuu, Meelis. "Cold War Show Trials in Estonia: Justice and Propaganda in the Balance." Accessed February 14, 2019. http://www.mnemosyne.ee/old/wp-content/uploads/2015/04/Meelis_Maripuu_-_Cold_War_Show_Trials_in_Estonia.pdf.

Maripuu, Meelis. "The Execution of Estonian Jews in the Local Detention Institutions in 1941-1942." Accessed October 12, 2022. https://muuseum.jewish ee/history/Holocaust/Estonia%201940-45 eng.pdf.

"Martin Sandberger." Wikipedia. Accessed January 6, 2019. https://en.wikipedia.org/wiki/Martin Sandberger.

Mayr, Walter. "The Quiet Death of a Nazi: Martin Sandberger's Last, and Only Interview," *Spiegel Online* (April 15, 2010). Accessed January 9, 2019. http://www.spiegel.de/international/germany/the-quiet-death-of-a-nazi-martin-sandberger-s-last-and-only-interview-a-687922-2.html,

Memory and Conscience Conference 2016. "Viljandi." Accessed August 5, 2020. https://www.memoryandconscience.eu/conference2016-viljandi/.

"Molotov-Ribbentrop Pact." Wikipedia. Accessed January 24, 2019. https://en.wikipedia.org/wiki/Molotov%E2%80%93Ribbentrop Pact.

Moorhouse, Roger. *The Devil's Alliance: Hitler's Pact with Stalin. 1939-1941* (New York: Basic Books, 2014). Accessed September 17, 2018.https://books.google.com/books?id=Nz RAwAAQBAJ&pg=RA1-PT163&lpg=RA1-PT163&dq=serov+instructions&source=bl&ots=X RoUp2pZp&sig=6LT1l8Co1POocjN13KSIwUeGo20&hl=en&sa=X&ved=2ahUKEwihhNyt7MLdAhVB3IMKHbwYDfEQ

6AEwEHoECAAQAQ#v=onepage&q=serov%20
instructions&f=false.

Mourning the Ancients. "Dr. Martin Sandberger." Interview,
1991. Accessed January 30, 2021. http://www.
mourningtheancient.com/ww2-x24.htm.

Museum Dungeons of the KGB. *Crimes of Communism and
the Struggle for Estonia's Freedom.* Tartu: Estonian
American Fund for Economic Education, 2006.
Accessed July 21, 2019. https://www.eafund.org/pdf/
KGB_Dungeons_Tartu.pdf.

"Nacht und Nebel." Wikipedia. Accessed September 30,
2021.https://en.wikipedia.org/wiki/Nacht_und_
Nebel.

National WWII Museum. "Operation Barbarossa: The
Biggest of All Time." Accessed June 18, 2021.
https://www.nationalww2museum.org/war/articles/
operation-barbarosAsa

Nazi Conspiracy and Aggression. "Document L-180: Report
by Stahlecker on the Activities of Einsatzgruppe
A until October 15, 1941," vol. VII (Washington:
U.S. Government Printing Office, 1946): 978-996.
Accessed August 14, 2019. http://defendinghistory.
com/wp-content/uploads/2015/01/Partial-
Translation-of-2nd-Stahlecker-Report-.pdf.

Niitsoo, Viktor. "The Nonviolent Resistance to the Soviet Occupation in the First Soviet Year of Estonia in 1940-1941." Accessed August 11, 2021. https://www.academia.edu/36188889/The_nonviolent_resistance_to_the_Soviet_occupation_in_the_first_Soviet_year_of_Estonia_in_1940_1941.

Niitsoo, Viktor. "Unarmed Resistance in the Years 1940-41. Algus Tuna 1/2001. Accessed August 11, 2021. https://www.ra.ee/wp-content/uploads/2017/03/NiitsooViktor_Relvastamata_V_TUNA2002_1.pdf.

Nuremberg Military Tribunals. "Trials of War Criminals Before the Nuremberg Military Tribunals, Volume IV. The Einsatzgruppen Case." Accessed September 1, 2020. https://www.loc.gov/rr/frd/Military_Law/pdf/NT_war-criminals_Vol-IV.pdf.

"Occupation of the Baltic States." Wikipedia. Accessed June 1, 2020. https://en.wikipedia.org/wiki/Occupation_of_the_Baltic_states.

"Operation Barbarossa." Wikipedia. Accessed January 12, 2023. https://en.wikipedia.org/wiki/Operation_Barbarossa.

"Operation Priboi." Wikipedia. Accessed July 19, 2019. https://en.wikipedia.org/wiki/Operation_Priboi.

Piir, Enno. *Sakalamaa Ei Unusta, Viljandi Linn*. Viljandi, Estonia: Memento Viljandi Ühendus, Viljandimaa Muinsuskaitse Ühendus, Viljandi Muuseum, 1997.

Puttsepp, Juhani. "How Many People Were Killed by the Shooters of the Tartu Concentration Camp in 1941 and 1944?" *Postimees* (September 17, 2001). Accessed September 15, 2020. https://tartu.postimees. ee/1891679/kui-palju-inimesi-tapsid-tartu-koonduslaagri-mahalaskjad-1941-1944.

Röngelep, Major Riho and Brigadier General Michale Hesslholt Clemmesen. "Tartu in the 1941 Summer War." *Baltic Defence Review*, no. 9, vol. 1/2005. Accessed September 3, 2021. https://www.baltdefcol. org/files/docs/bdreview/bdr-2003-9-13.pdf.

Roberts, Geoffrey. *Molotov: Stalin's Cold Warrior* (Potomac Books, 2011). Accessed March 29, 2019. https:// books.google.com/books?id=eGR--KVel4UC&pg=P A2&lpg=PA2&dq=molotov+nyet&source=bl&ots=t5l bwz2s7q&sig=ACfU3U04EWB4eGynsWeAj2u8DZ cR_dSPsw&hl=en&sa=X&ved=2ahUKEwjenvyR4aX hAhWh3YMKHRdZBRgQ6AEwEnoECAoQAQ# v=onepage&q=molotov%20nyet&f=false.

Royde-Smith, John Graham. "Operation Barbarossa." Accessed August 5, 2020. https://www.britannica. com/event/Operation-Barbarossa/Later-actions.

Smith, David James, Artis Pabriks, Thomas Lane and Aldis Purs. *The Baltic States: Estonia, Latvia and Lithuania* (Psychology Press, 2002). Accessed July 28, 2019. https://books.google.com/books?id=YaYbzQQN97 EC&pg=PA35&lpg=PA35&dq=Hjalmar+Mae&sou rce=bl&ots=WT5ZSPR96C&sig=ACfU3U0vF_Yof 4YdBxTRJkpXQXossAWCeQ&hl=en&sa=X&ved= 2ahUKEwiMz6eul9bjAhWSGs0KHZYuAmQ4Ch DoATADegQJCRAB#v=onepage&q=Hjalmar%20 Mae&f=false.

Smoltczyk, Alexander. "Helping Europe's War Dead Find a Final Resting Place," *Spiegel Online* (May 7, 2015). Accessed September 7, 2019. https://www.spiegel.de/ international/germany/bones-of-world-war-soldiers-still-being-excavated-across-europe-a-1029530.html.

Snyder, Timothy. *Bloodlands, Europe between Hitler and Stalin* New York: Basic Books, 2010.

"Soviet Deportations from Estonia." Wikipedia. Accessed February 17, 2019. https://en.wikipedia.org/wiki/ Soviet_deportations_from_Estonia.

"Soviet Repressions of Polish Citizens (1939-1946)." Wikipedia. Accessed June 17, 2020. https:// en.wikipedia.org/wiki/Soviet_repressions_of_Polish_ citizens_(1939%E2%80%931946).

Stafford, Tom. "The Mass Surrender of German Troops
    to the 347th Infantry Regiment on May 6,
    1945"(August 17, 2004). Accessed March 14, 2019.
    http://87thinfantrydivision.com/tom-stafford/the-
    mass-surrender-of-german-troops-to-the-347th-
    infantry-regiment-on-may-6-1945,

Stepanov, Sergei. "Veteran Security Officer Sentenced,"
    The Baltic Times (November 7, 2002). Accessed July
    19, 2019. https://m.baltictimes.com/article/jcms/
    id/107147/.

Stevick, E. Doyle. "The Politics of the Holocaust in Estonia:
    Historical Memory and Social Divisions in Estonian
    Education," *Journal of Burmese Scholarship* (November
    15, 2008): 217-244. Accessed September 15, 2019.
    https://journalofburmesescholarship.org/pprs/
    Stevick-HistoricalMemory.pdf.

"Tallinn Offensive." Wikipedia. Accessed March 27, 2021.
    https://en.wikipedia.org/wiki/Tallinn_offensive.

Tambur, Silver. "A Memorial to the Victims of Communism
    Opens in Estonia," *Estonian World* (August 23, 2018).
    Accessed September 9, 2019. https://estonianworld.
    com/life/memorial-to-the-victims-of-communism-
    opens-in-estonia/.

Tamme, Tuudor. "These Acts Are to Blame – the Massacre
    on Scheel's Plot," *Kultuur ja Elu.* Accessed September
    13, 2019. http://kultuur.elu.ee/ke490_shceel.htm.

https://kultuur-elu-ee.translate.goog/ke490_shceel.
htm?_x_tr_sch=http&_x_tr_sl=et&_x_tr_tl=en&_x_
tr_hl=en&_x_tr_pto=sc.

Tarm, Michael. "Stalin Agent Found Guilty in Estonia," *The
Independent* (November 1, 2002). Accessed July 19,
2019. https://www.independent.co.uk/news/world/
europe/stalin-agent-found-guilty-in-estonia-125977.
html.

Taylor, Frederick. "How Many Died in the Bombing of
Dresden?" *Spiegel Online* (October 2, 2008). Accessed
March 20, 2019. http://www.spiegel.de/international/
germany/death-toll-debate-how-many-died-in-the-
bombing-of-dresden-a-581992.html.

The Baltic Times. "Nazi War Crimes in Estonia
Documented." May 3, 2001. Accessed September
23, 2021. https://www.baltictimes.com/news/
articles/4903/.

The Baltic Way. 1989-2014. "History." Accessed July 4, 2021.
https://www.thebalticway.eu/en/history/.

"The Bombing of Dresden." Wikipedia. Accessed June 11,
2021. https://en.wikipedia.org/wiki/Bombing_of_
Dresden_in_World_War_II.

The History Learning Site. "The Bombing of Dresden."
Accessed June 12, 2021. https://en.wikipedia.org/
wiki/Bombing_of_Dresden_in_World_War_II.

"The Holocaust in Estonia." Wikia.org. Accessed September 29, 2021. https://military.wikia.org/wiki/The_Holocaust_in_Estonia.

"The Holocaust in Estonia." Wikipedia. Accessed February 2, 2019. https://en.wikipedia.org/wiki/The_Holocaust_in_Estonia.

Thomason, Ian. "When Tallinn Burned – Estonia Commemorates the March 1944 Bombings." *Estonian World* (March 9, 2022). Accessed March 11, 2022. https://estonianworld.com/security/when-tallinn-burned-estonia-commemorates-the-march-1944-bombings/?fbclid=IwAR1LOZtkv6B0F2V2ctTAprAMD-yk7959-pTMt0IZf5svDZHJlGa6lyc5WBo.

"Timeline of Estonian History." Wikipedia. Accessed June 20, 2020. https://en.wikipedia.org/wiki/Timeline_of_Estonian_history.

Toth, Sara. "Russia Condemns Partisan Trial Underway in Valga Court," *The Baltic Times* (August 29, 2002). Accessed July 19, 2019. https://m.baltictimes.com/article/jcms/id/106845/.

Traces of War. "German War Graves Dorpat/Tartu." Accessed September 30, 2020. https://www.tracesofwar.com/sights/3627/German-War-Graves-Dorpat---Tartu.htm.

Traces of War. "Martin Sandberger." Accessed January 9, 2019. https://www.tracesofwar.com/articles/4748/ Sandberger-Martin.htm?c=gw.

The University of Tartu. https://ut.ee/en.

UPI Archives. "Profiles of the 21 Nazi Leaders on Trial at Nuremberg." (September 30, 1946). Accessed March 27, 2019. http://avalon.law.yale.edu/imt/03-28-46. asp.

U.S. Central Intelligence Agency. "Estonian War Crimes Trial." Declassified Memo 2004. Accessed January 6, 2019. https://www.cia.gov/library/readingroom/docs/ LINNAS%2C%20KARL 0016.pdf.

U.S. Court of Appeals for the Second Circuit. "Karl Linnas, Petitioner, v. Immigration & Naturalization Service, Respondent, 790 F.2d 1024 (2d Cir. 1986) Argued March 17, 1986, Decided May 8, 1985. Accessed December 28, 2018. https://law.justia.com/cases/ federal/appellate-courts/F2/790/1024/8258.

U. S. Department of State, Office of the Historian. "Foreign Relations of The United States

Diplomatic Papers, 1941, General, The Soviet Union, volume I," 860I.00/467. Accessed September 18, 2018. https://history.state.gov/historicaldocuments/ frus1941v01/d627.

U.S. District Court for the Eastern District of New York. "United States v. Linnas, 527 F. Supp. 426 (EDNY 1981)." (July 30, 1981). Accessed December 28, 2018. https://law.justia.com/cases/federal/district-courts/FSupp/527/426/2369427/.

U.S. Holocaust Memorial Museum. "Invasion of the Soviet Union, June 1941." Accessed July 4, 2019. https://encyclopedia.ushmm.org/content/en/article/invasion-of-the-soviet-union-june-1941.

Viljandi Uudiseia. "Dr. Jaan Vares 50. Aastane." *Sakala,* no. 8 (January 20, 1939). Accessed April 15, 2021. https://dea.digar.ee/cgi-bin/dea?a=d&d=sakala ew19390120.2.27.

"Vyacheslav Molotov." Wikipedia. Accessed January 24, 2019. https://en.wikipedia.org/wiki/Vyacheslav Molotov.

"War Crimes Trials in Soviet Estonia." Wikipedia. Accessed September 18, 2020. https://en.wikipedia.org/wiki/War_crimes_trials_in_Soviet_Estonia.

"War Crimes Trials in Soviet Estonia." Wikiwand. Accessed October 15, 2020. https://www.wikiwand.com/en/War_crimes_trials_in_Soviet_Estonia.

Weiss-Wendt, Anton. *On the Margins: Essays on the History of Jews in Estonia.*

Budapest, Hungary: Central European University Press, 2017. Accessed July 15, 2019.

"World War II Casualties." Wikipedia. Accessed June 20, 2021. https://en.wikipedia.org/wiki/World_War_II_casualties.

Wreck Site. "MV Moero, 1944." Accessed August 14, 2018. https://wrecksite.eu/wreck.aspx?15307.

Yasmann, Victor. "Russia: Using Racism is a Time-Honored Kremlin Tool," *Radio Free Europe* (June 19, 2006). Accessed January 8, 2019. https://www.rferl.org/a/1069290.html.

Zeller, Tom Jr. "The Nuremberg Hangings – Not So Smooth Either." *The New York Times* (January 17, 2007). Accessed March 27, 2019. https://thelede.blogs.nytimes.com/2007/01/17/the-nuremburg-hangings-not-so-smooth-either/.

Acknowledgements

Many people have helped me during my journey to discover my family's Estonian history. I owe a debt of gratitude to my writing community at the University of California-Riverside where I earned an MFA as well as to the Lighthouse Writers Workshop in Denver, Colorado.

Many thanks to Tod Goldberg, David Ulin and Gina Frangello. I am also grateful to Annette Davis and Laura Jo Brunson, my writing colleagues, who read many early chapters of this book and helped to copy-edit the manuscript in its final form.

Throughout my quest to connect with my Estonian heritage, my brother, Michael, who lives in Estonia has been one of my strongest supporters. With his help, I accessed invaluable family records from the Estonian National Archives and was also able to learn more about the vibrant country Estonia has become. My brother, Jim, and my sister, Tina, also cheered me along as I completed multiple versions of our family's story.

Finally, I appreciate the many beta readers who provided useful comments on earlier drafts of this book and encouraged me to share my family's narrative with a broader audience of readers. I could not have completed this project without the love and generous support provided by my husband, Paul, who has always believed in me over the many years I devoted to writing this book.

Questions and Topics for Discussion

1. Like Latvia and Lithuania, Estonia has a complicated and often tragic history. What combination of courage and stubbornness allowed these Baltic countries to preserve their unique identities while they were occupied over the centuries?

2. Many survivors from World War II have chosen not to talk about the trauma they experienced. What are the benefits that families might gain from remembering and preserving their wartime narratives?

3. During their respective occupations, both the Soviet Union and Germany imposed their legal systems on Estonia. Since Bruno's activities were defined as treasonous by both countries, what should have been his punishment?

4. After Estonia regained its independence, Estonian prosecutors began war crime trials to investigate the crimes against humanity that occurred during World War II. Did these judicial proceedings help Estonia to recapture a history that was suppressed while the country was occupied by the Soviet Union?

5. Throughout Europe, German officials have created stumbling stones to honor those who were victimized under the Nazi regime. What purpose do these efforts to identify the names of individual wartime victims serve?

6. What can we learn by exploring the history of the family members who came before us? What responsibility do we have to keep their memory alive?

Kaia Gallagher is a Denver-based author who enjoys writing narrative nonfiction, personal essays, and flash fiction. In addition to having an MFA in Creative Writing from the University of California-Riverside, Kaia earned a Ph.D. in Sociology from Brown University.

A long-time Book Club fan, Kaia welcomes opportunities to connect with reader groups.

Connect with Kaia at
https://www.kaiagallagher.com
Instagram: @kgall007
Email: kaia@kaiagallagher.com

If you enjoyed reading her family memoir, please post a review on your favorite book review site.

For monthly book recommendations, sign up for Kaia's newsletter at www.kaiagallagher.com

www.ingramcontent.com/pod-product-compliance
Lightning Source LLC
Chambersburg PA
CBHW071144130626
46553CB00004B/1518